GLOUCESTER

HISTORY YOU CAN SEE

GLOUCESTER

HISTORY YOU CAN SEE

D.G. AMPHLETT

First published 2015

The History Press
The Mill, Brimscombe Port
Stroud, Gloucestershire, GL5 2QG
www.thehistorypress.co.uk

British Library Cataloguing in Publication Data.
A catalogue record for this book is available from the British Library.

ISBN 978 0 7524 7017 7

Typesetting and origination by The History Press
Printed in Great Britain

Main cover image:
W. Lloyd MacKenzie, via Flickr
www.flickr.com/photos/saffron_blaze

Contents

INTRODUCTION

GLOUCESTER IS situated on the east side of the River Severn and historically – until the construction of the Severn Railway Bridge, at Sharpness, in 1879 – was the lowest bridging, or fording, point of the river. Its strategic importance was recognised by the Romans who established a fortress and, later, a colony here.

Gloucester also grew as a significant religious centre in the medieval period. The history of the cathedral can be traced back to around AD 679, when Hwice, subregulus of Mercia, founded a minster. The translation of the bones of St Oswald to Gloucester in AD 909 made Gloucester a place of pilgrimage and the interring of King Edward II's remains in St Peter's Abbey (the present-day cathedral) considerably enhanced its reputation. Under Norman patronage, the abbey flourished; it continued to grow and has left Gloucester a magnificent cathedral. Religious houses expanded greatly during the Middles Ages, especially with the arrival of the friars in the thirteenth century, and Llanthony Priory, an Augustinian house, would become one of the wealthiest religious houses in the kingdom by the sixteenth century.

Following the Dissolution, Gloucester Cathedral was created from St Peter's Abbey. Its second bishop, John Hooper, would be martyred during the reign of Mary I and the site of his martyrdom is commemorated by Edward W. Thornhill's imposing statue in St Mary's Square, created in 1862. William Laud, Dean of Gloucester Cathedral (1616–21), was a controversial figure who reversed a number of Puritan innovations. His mark has also been left on the cathedral, for he was responsible for railing in the altar at the east end. These communion rails can now be seen in the Lady chapel.

This book aims to tell some of the stories of the people who lived in Gloucester. Numbered amongst these is Robert Raikes (1735–1811), who established and popularised Sunday schools, and numerous monuments dedicated to his achievements are located around Gloucester. Also to feature is James Wood, the eccentric banker who gained a reputation for such miserliness that he is said to have inspired Charles Dickens' character Ebenezer Scrooge. More recently, Gloucester was also the birthplace of Hubert Cecil Booth (1871–1955), the inventor of the vacuum cleaner, and was the place where the first British jet-powered aircraft made its short hop along the runway that existed at Hucclecote.

Gloucester is also well known for its beautiful nineteenth-century inland port,

established when a ship canal linked the port to Sharpness, allowing seagoing vessels an easier passage to reach Gloucester. Careful preservation of many of the buildings during the latter part of the twentieth century has ensured that the site is remarkably complete.

The arrangement of the material in this book is roughly chronological, starting with the Roman period and travelling through to the twentieth century.

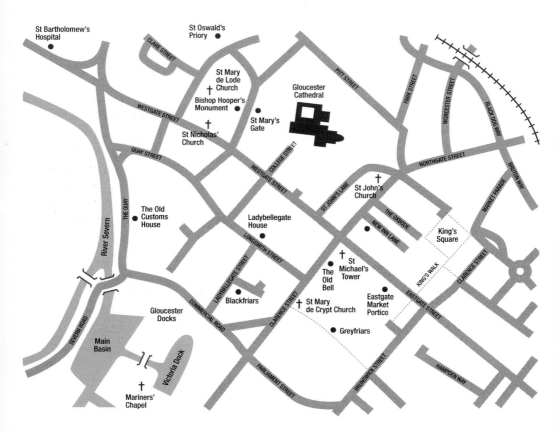

Map of central Gloucester.

One

The Arrival of the Romans and the Establishment of Glevum

IN THE SUMMER of AD 43, Roman legionary and auxillary soldiers landed on the Kentish coast. This expeditionary force was made up of 40–50,000 men, headed by Aulus Plautius. The army made its way towards Colchester, pausing to allow for the arrival of Emperor Claudius, who then led the victorious troops into Colchester, thus enabling the emperor to gain the maximum political advantage from the expansion of the empire. It is likely that Claudius received the surrender of several of Britain's tribes during this time.

One of these tribes may have been the Dobunni, whose tribal kingdom included the area covered by present-day Gloucestershire.

Within a few years, the Roman Army controlled most of the southern and eastern parts of Britain. A frontier zone, marking the edge of Roman influence in Britain in the AD 40s, ran from the Humber Estuary to the Severn Estuary, continuing south-westwards towards Lyme Bay. For much of the length of this frontier zone, a road, known as the Fosse Way, allowed for the swift deployment of troops and supplies.

Ermin Street

Gloucester's strategic importance as the lowest bridging point on the River Severn, led to the establishment of a Roman fort at Kingsholm within five years of the initial Roman invasion of Britain in AD 43. The fort at Kingsholm undoubtedly served as a base from which the Welsh tribes could be conquered and subdued. The Roman settlement at Gloucester (Glevum) was served by a number of Roman roads to enable the transportation of foodstuffs, arms and men. From Glevum, a road traversed due south to Abone, the Roman ferry station at Sea Mills, on the banks of the River Avon. A causeway also connected Glevum to territories west of the River Severn, including the Roman fort

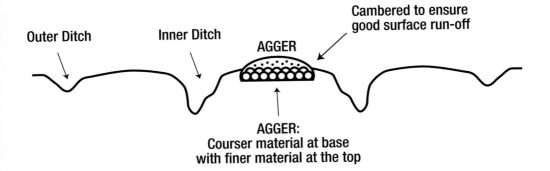

Diagram showing the typical cross-section of a Roman Road.

at Caerleon, and Ermin Street linked Glevum with Silchester (in present-day Hampshire). Ermin Street — the name and alignment of which still survives along much of the route today — is easily identified from the landscape, owing to the relative straightness with which the Romans built their roads.

Although Roman roads are often thought of as straight, this is only true in part. Sometimes the terrain necessitated a deviation from the straight course. On the stretch of Ermin Street from Cirencester to Gloucester, a small adjustment to the north is made, keeping the road on higher ground and successfully avoiding several deep valleys by Syde and Brimpsfield. At Birdlip, the road deviates to the west and, in order to negotiate Birdlip Hill, the road zigzags to ease the descent on to Great Witcombe, at the foot of the hill. Ermin Street continues directly to Gloucester and on to Wooton Pitch. Here, a turn westwards is made to the northern gate of the city, along what is now London Road, for approximately 1 mile. This turn indicates that the founding of Glevum, as a colony for retired soldiers, took

place to the south of the original Roman fortress, which was built half a mile to the north of the city.

The Romans preferred high ground in the construction of their roads and, where practicable, the road as constructed in the following manner. More likely than not, the area for the road would have been covered by trees. This would have to be cleared — by felling the trees and burning the wood — to a width of 90ft (27m). At the edges of the clearing, parallel outer ditches would be constructed. Through the centre of the clearing, two more parallel ditches were dug to a width of 30ft (9m). An embankment would be built up between these two ditches, leaving a wide depression along one or both sides of the road. On top of the embankment, the road was metalled. This meant that a foundation layer of large stones was laid, followed by smaller stones, flints or gravel. Archaeologists refer to this embankment, which carried the road 'metal', as the agger. The surface was cambered to ensure good drainage. The above diagram summarises the typical construction of Roman roads.

The East Gate

Outside Boots in Eastgate Street, is a viewing platform which shows the Roman and medieval foundations of the East Gate. The Roman city of Glevum, constructed during the latter half of the first century, was approximately square with gatehouses in the centre of each of its four walls. These walls underwent a series of rebuilds over the following millennium, with work carried out in the tenth century by Aethelfaeda, daughter of Alfred the Great; repairs in the eleventh century under the Normans; and further work to repair the damage resulting from the Barons' War in the thirteenth century. The military importance of Gloucester had declined considerably by the sixteenth century and alternative uses were sought for the buildings. In 1584, part of the East Gate was turned into a women's prison. In 1703, a school for poor children was established.

Viewing platform of the East Gate remains.

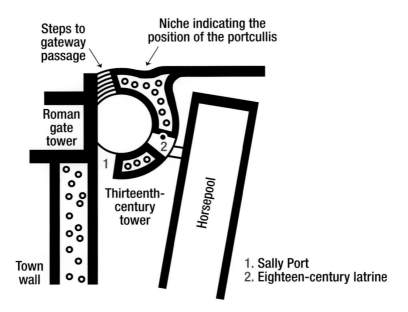

Sketch plan of the East Gate remains.

In 1643, the Royalists attempted to tunnel under the moat in order to blow up the gatehouse. The endeavour was unsuccessful and their tunnel became flooded, owing to the high water table (*see* Gloucester and the English Civil War p. 69). The East Gate was demolished in 1778, to enable the widening of the road.

From street level, looking down through the viewing platform, the foundations of the thirteenth-century south tower can be seen. At its north west, steps from the tower once led to the gateway passage. To the south west there is a blocked sally port, whilst to the south east, an eighteenth-century latrine has been inserted. On the north side of the tower, it is possible to see a niche indicating the position of the portcullis. To the west of this semi-circular tower lies the southern section of the second-century square gate towers; to the south are the remains of the fourth-century Roman wall (much rebuilt during the thirteenth century); and to the east a cobbled and walled horse pool was constructed in the sixteenth century.

Emperor Nerva Statue

On Southgate Street, opposite the Eastgate Street Shopping Centre, stands a statue of Emperor Nerva, who is regarded, in some quarters, as being the founder of Glevum (Gloucester). Certainly Gloucester seems to have come into being during Nerva's sixteen-month reign in AD 97. The statue, sculpted by Anthony Stones and cast at Pangolin's Foundry, Chalford, was erected by the Gloucester Civic Trust in 2002.

The Emperor Nerva statue,
Southgate Street,
sculpted by Anthony Stones.

A stainless-steel time capsule has been placed in the statue's hollow plinth. It contains items relating to the foundation of Roman Gloucester up to the present day. Although Nerva was in his sixties (old by Roman standards) when he became emperor, the statue depicts him as a younger man on horseback.

Nerva, the son of a wealthy Roman lawyer, was born, in AD 35, in Narnia, located 50 miles to the north of Rome. For much of his life, Nerva held a series of political positions and was able to maintain high office, despite changes of regime. In AD 65, Emperor Nero awarded him special honours for helping to suppress the conspiracy of Piso, in AD 71 he was chosen as consul by Vespasian, and in AD 90 he also served as consul to Domitian. During the latter years of Domitian's reign, the emperor came to be regarded as a tyrant, with many senators, knights and imperial officials exiled or executed. This culminated in his murder and Nerva accepted the role of emperor. After Domitian's tyranny, Nerva was popular with the senate. He was regarded as a benevolent ruler and embarked upon a modest programme of public works, repairing roads and aqueducts.

Nerva did, however, have trouble restoring law and order following Domitian's death. Popular resentment resulted in the destruction of his statues and the demolition of his ceremonial arches. Nerva was also unpopular with the army.

In AD 97, the praetorian guard mutinied and Nerva was imprisoned in the imperial palace. The guard demanded the surrender of Petronius and Parthenius, the people responsible for Domitian's death. Nerva resisted these demands with a degree of personal courage, even baring his own throat to the soldiers. In the end, however, this brave gesture was in vain and the praetorian guards captured the two men, who were put to death. Petronius was killed by a single sword blow, whilst Parthenius met a particularly gruesome end. His genitals were cut off and shoved into his mouth before his throat was cut. Nerva emerged unharmed after the incident, but clearly his authority had been compromised. Nerva remained childless and therefore adopted Marcus Ulpius Traianus (Trajan) as his son and heir. Trajan was governor of Upper Germany, a respected man who could command the support of the army and the senate. This move meant that Nerva was able to live out his final months in peace and allowed him to gain the reputation as a wise and peaceful ruler. He died on 28 January AD 98.

Other Roman Artefacts

In the window of the HSBC Bank, Westgate Street, part of the base of a Roman column has been put on display. It was found during excavations carried out in the area in 1971. The stone supported a large Roman column measuring nearly 10m high, which is now in the city museum. It is believed to date from approximately AD 120–150, when the Roman forum was built. A Lewis hole near the top of the slab was intended for lifting purposes. The slab, of oolitic limestone, was quarried from Leckhampton. In the Eastgate Market, a section of mosaic pavement has also been put on display. It is believed to have come from a substantial Roman house and was discovered during the construction of a new market during the 1960s.

Two

MEDIEVAL GLOUCESTER: THE CATHEDRAL AND ITS ENVIRONS

GLOUCESTER CATHEDRAL is one of six former abbey churches that became cathedrals under Henry VIII following the Dissolution of the Monasteries. (The others were Bristol, Oxford, Peterborough, Chester and, temporarily, Westminster.) The cathedral can trace its origins back to 679, when a minster church was founded by Osric, sub-King of Hwice, from lands given by King Ethelred of Mercia. It was founded as a religious house of monks and nuns who lived separately but worshipped together and was ruled by an abbess, Osric's sister, Kynburga. For the next 400 years little is known about the communities that worshipped within the minster. It is believed that Benedictine rule was established in around 1016.

Norman historians looked back to the time of St Bede and the monastic revival in the tenth century as being a golden age of monasticism. William of Malmsbury, writing in the twelfth century, wrote that 'the zeal and religion had grown cold many years

before the coming of the Normans'. There is some evidence of this at Gloucester, and when Serlo, a close associate of William the Conqueror and a monk from Mont St Michel, Normandy, was appointed abbot in 1072, the monastery consisted of only two monks and eight novices. By 1100, the numbers had grown to over sixty monks. After the Conquest, the Normans embarked upon the building and rebuilding of many churches and monasteries, and Gloucester Abbey was certainly part of that growth. Another impetus to the rebuilding by Serlo was the damage caused to the abbey in 1088, during the civil war concerning the royal succession. William II's response was to ensure that Gloucester Abbey received a great deal of support and granted many estates to it from himself and his barons. Consequently, the abbey did not face further unrest during the Anglo-Norman period. Under Serlo's leadership, the abbey grew in importance as a centre of spirituality, the rebuilding of which has left behind a very impressive building.

Gloucester Cathedral.

The most striking feature of Abbot Serlo's new building is the nave with its huge cylindrical columns. The third pillar of the Norman arcade, on the south side, leans to the south owing to the presence of the soft infill of a Roman defensive ditch below its foundations. This has also caused the south wall to lean outwards, which at one point is 11in (28cm) out of line. In 1122, the abbey was severely damaged by fire and the calcination is still visible on the nave piers. The stone-ribbed vault of the nave was built in 1242, along with the roof above, which used 110 oak trees felled from the Royal Forest of Dean, given to the abbey by Henry III.

The accession of Edward III (reign 1327–77) is the starting point for the construction of perpendicular architecture in the cathedral. In the south transept, the south window is the oldest surviving perpendicular window, dating from around 1335. The cloisters, begun after 1351, possess the earliest surviving example of a large-scale fan vaulting.

Shortly after 1450, Abbot Seabroke rebuilt the central tower. The final alterations to the cathedral were completed in around 1482 and involved the rebuilding of the Lady chapel. St Peter's Abbey became Gloucester Cathedral on 3 September 1541 and its royal connections may have been a factor in the creation of this new bishopric. The first bishop was John Wakeman, the last abbot of Tewkesbury Abbey, and the second was John Hooper, who was burned at the stake in 1555 for his zealous Protestant beliefs.

The cathedral managed to survive the religious upheavals of the seventeenth century. In 1616, William Laud was appointed Dean of Gloucester and his many High Church principles caused concern to the then bishop, Miles Smith. The damage inflicted during the English Civil War was minimal, but during the Commonwealth a move was made to demolish the great edifice. Fortunately, the timely intervention of the mayor and burgesses secured its future.

Nineteenth-century restoration was, in the main, tactful. F.S. Waller began work on the cathedral in 1847, with George Gilbert Scott's ornate reredos in the presbytery being the principle Victorian addition. Created in 1872–73, the reredos' sculpted figures (carved by James Redfern) depict the Nativity, Ascension and Deposition. Christopher Whall reglazed the Lady chapel in 1898 and it remains an important work dating from the Arts and Crafts Movement.

The Cathedral

The Nave

The huge Norman piers, dating from the time of Abbot Serlo's rebuilding, dominate the nave. These columns are some 7ft (2.13m) in diameter, and 32ft (9.75m) high.

At the east end of the nave, a stone choir screen – on which the organ was placed – dates from 1823 and was designed by Robert Smirke. The organ case here was created by Thomas Harris and dates from 1665. Another organ case, which stands on the east side of the choir screen, is thought to be even earlier and probably dates from about 1640, by Robert Dalham. The organ pipes were painted by John Campion with heraldic designs.

The nave.

The Cloisters

The cloisters, to the north of the nave, are rightly described as 'the most memorable in England'. The earliest part, which connects the nave to the chapter house, was begun during the abbacy of Thomas Horton, who resided there between 1351–77. Here we also see evidence of the earliest surviving fan vaulting, thought to have been constructed between about 1351–60. The chapter house dates from the late eleventh century and, during monastic times, this was where the monks would meet daily to discuss and regulate the life of the abbey.

The south side of the cloisters contains twenty carrels (cubicles), which were used by the monks for writing and studying. Each carrel would have contained a desk and a stool. The north walk contains the fan-vaulted lavatorium at the west end and is lit

The cloisters.

by eight two-light windows. This was, as the name implies, where the monks washed and about half the width of the lavatorium is taken up with a stone ledge and trough. Originally, this carried a lead tank from which the water, piped to the abbey from the springs of Robinswood Hill, came out of spigots. Opposite the lavatorium is a two-bay opening to a recess, where the towels were hung. Along the north wall there is a stone bench with traces of games that the novice monks may have played, including Nine Men's Morris and Fox and Geese.

The Choir

The choir stalls, which have occupied the crossing since roughly 1350–60, are particularly fine examples, with their ogee-arched canopies and a series of forty-four misericords. The main documentary source for the medieval work carried out at the abbey is the *Historia Monasterii Petri Gloucestriae*, compiled by Walter Fraucester, who was abbot from 1381–1412. Fraucester's *Historia* often assigns work carried out at the abbey to a particular abbacy. In the case of the choir stalls, those on the north side are ascribed to Abbot de Staunton, meaning that they were constructed prior to 1351, while those on the south side are ascribed to Abbot Horton and therefore date from after 1351. The misericords depict scenes from folk tales, domesticity, legendary creatures, and some scenes from the Bible. The scenes include: Samson and Delilah, the flight of Alexander, youths gambling, Balaam and his donkey, a mermaid, and three shepherds following a star. The stalls were restored by Sir George Gilbert Scott, 1869–79, when he also added a further fourteen misericords.

The Presbytery

Much of what remains here resulted from the restoration carried out by Scott. Of particular note is the 1872–73 ornate reredos depicting the Nativity, Ascension and Deposition (Christ being taken down from the cross). The brass lectern is an early design by J.P. Bentley, which was made by Hart & Son and displayed at the 1862 exhibition. The lectern depicts an eagle seizing a dragon and the circular base is supported on six eagle's claws grasping balls. The lectern was given to Gloucester Cathedral by J.C. Dent in 1866.

The Great East Window

The Great East Window, which lights the presbytery and choir, is one of the largest Gothic medieval windows built. It is 72ft (21.91m) high and 38ft (11.6m) wide. The window was glazed in around 1350–60 using, almost entirely, white, blue, yellow and red glass. The overall theme of the window might best be described as the 'Coronation of the Blessed Virgin and Christ in Majesty', with both Christ and the Virgin Mary given a prominent place in the scene. At the very top of the window, a fifteenth-century insertion shows St Clement enthroned as a pope. In the central six lights are tall canopies, below which is a row of angels. The second light of this row is another fifteenth-century insertion, showing the Virgin and Child. Below this, on the first full tier, the crowned Virgin Mary, with a crowned Christ, are in the centre, flanked on either side by the twelve apostles. The next tier, below, shows a number of male and female saints, including St George, St Margaret and St Lawrence. Next, a row of alternating male and female saints is depicted with the figures turning towards each other. The following tier has bishops and abbots, with three

The Great East Window.

The Tower

The massive central tower was mostly built during the abbacy of Thomas Seabroke and dates from roughly 1451–57. It stands some 225ft (68.6m) high and contains a ring of twelve bells. In addition, the cathedral tower is home to England's only remaining medieval bourdon or 'great bell'. The diameter of the bell measures 68.5in and it weighs 59cwt 3qr 14lb. The bell carries an inscription which reads: 'ME FECIT FIERI CONVENTUS NOMINE PETRI', that is, 'The convent had me cast in the name of Peter'. Between each word of the inscription are the arms of the abbey. The bell founder is unknown, although his marks can be found on the bell.

kings in the centre, the first of which may be Edward II. Below this, the stained glass depicts a range of heraldry. In 1861–62, the entire window was taken down and re-leaded.

The Whispering Gallery

When the Great East Window was built during the fourteenth century, the east and west galleries were separated. The fourteenth-century solution was to build a bridge that ran behind the window – yet without obscuring the light reaching it – to connect the galleries. Today this is known at the 'Whispering Gallery', so-called as sound travels readily along through the passage. So, if one person whispered into the entrance to this gallery, the other person, standing at the other entrance to the gallery, should be able to hear clearly what is being said.

The cathedral tower.

The Lady Chapel

The Lady chapel was built in around 1465–82 and was the last medieval phase of construction on the abbey. Inside, the mutilated reredos, from about 1480, has been decorated with portraits of Christ by Ian McKillop. The east window contains fragments of medieval glass, assembled together in their present form during in the early nineteenth century. The chapel is also home to some of the most superb examples of stained glass from the Arts and Craft Movement, which were made between 1898 and 1924 by Christopher Whall. The lead font is one of only nine in Gloucestershire and came from St James' church in Lancaut, Tidenham, Gloucestershire. St James' church is a twelfth-century construction, which was abandoned in around 1865. The font was presented to the cathedral in 1940. The communion rails date from approximately 1617, when Laud (later archbishop) was Dean of Gloucester. Laud rejected a number of Puritan practices and began to reinstate communion tables at the east end of churches with communion rails in front of them.

The Lady chapel.

The South Porch

The porch was probably constructed in around 1430, during the abbacy of John Morwent – perhaps after the previous porch had suffered a partial collapse. It was much restored during 1868–70 and several statues, carved by James Redfern, were added. The statues are all in crocketed niches. Those above the entrance depict the four evangelists, along with St Peter and St Paul. From left to right (west to east), the statues are: St Matthew, St Mark, St Peter, St Paul, St Luke and St John. On the west side of the entrance arch is the statue of St King Osric, who founded a minster here in the seventh century. On the north side of the entrance arch is Serlo, Abbot of Gloucester from 1072–1104, who was responsible for

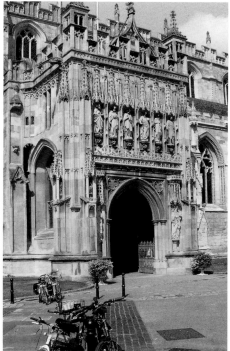

The South Porch.

much of the nave. In smaller niches, the four church fathers are depicted. On the west side of the porch, St Augustine is shown with a book in one hand and a flaming heart in the other (indicating his charity), while St Gregory is shown with a translation of scripture and a model of a church (indicating his support for the church). On the east side of the porch, St Jerome is shown with a book in one hand and a dove on his shoulder (the dove symbolising the Holy Spirit), and St Ambrose is shown singing – perhaps one of the compositions for which he was well known.

The Cathedral Precincts

Infirmary Arches

To the north of the cloisters are the ruins of the infirmary hall, which consist of the west end and south arcade. They date from the thirteenth century and survive, despite a demolition order for the infirmary hall in 1630, because they were incorporated into housing. The houses were cleared between 1831 and 1855, leaving the remains of the infirmary that can be seen today.

The Infirmary Arches.

St Mary's Gate

The Great Gate of the abbey is first recorded in 1190. The archway of the gate dates from the twelfth century. It survives mostly complete and was greatly restored by Waller & Son in the late 1920s. To the south of the gateway, a sixteenth-century timber-framed building was constructed on an existing thirteenth-century undercroft. Here the almoner of the abbey would have resided. Through the leaded window, next to the gate, are the remnants of an opening (albeit much enlarged), where alms of food were distributed to the poor.

St Mary's Gate.

St Edward's Gate

Only part of the western tower of the lych gate, which spanned a narrow lane leading from Westgate Street, now survives. The gateway gave access to the abbey's burial grounds and was built in the thirteenth century with money given by Edward I. In the sixteenth century, Abbot Parker added a stair turret on the north side. The room above the arch was removed in 1806 and the east tower taken down in 1892. On the south face of the building, a shield displays what is thought to be the arms of the abbey's founder, King Osric. This was fixed to the building after the shield was discovered in the cathedral close in 1828.

St Edward's Gate. (Courtesy of E.H. Amphlett)

No. 7 Millers Green

No. 7 Millers Green dates from roughly 1670, although the plain brick front and sash windows were added in the eighteenth century. From the mid-nineteenth century, the house has accommodated the cathedral organist and perhaps the best-known organist to live here was Samuel Sebastian Wesley (1810–76).

Wesley was the son of Samuel Wesley (1766–1837), and was given the name Sebastian after the well-known composer and organist, Johann Sebastian Bach. He gained his first cathedral organist appointment at Hereford and would later serve at Exeter, Leeds and Winchester cathedrals. From the mid-1850s, Wesley's time at Winchester Cathedral was an unhappy one after he became involved in the drawing up of a specification for the organ in St George's Hall, Liverpool. The musical press criticised its old-fashioned specification and a heated public debate ensued. Wesley was also receiving a number of reprimands for dereliction of duty owing to the presence of Henry Wray, a somewhat over-zealous precentor. It is perhaps no surprise that when the dean and chapter of Gloucester Cathedral asked Wesley to recommend a new organist, he recommended himself and subsequently held the position in Gloucester Cathedral from 1865 until his death in 1876. The move may hint at Wesley's somewhat prickly character, stemming from his inability to move with the times, but also from the lack of recognition that he felt he deserved. Another indication of Wesley's temperamental nature occurred whilst organist of Gloucester Cathedral. He was invited by Mrs Ellicot, the dean's wife, to accompany and conduct the College Ladies' Society Choir but at the first rehearsal – and after only a few bars had been sung – Wesley shouted 'Cats!', throwing his arms into the air and storming out.

Today, Wesley is known for a number of hymn tunes including 'Aurelia', often sung to S.J. Stone's hymn 'The Church's One Foundation' and 'Hereford', often sung to

No. 7 Millers Green.

Charles Wesley's hymn 'O Thou Who Camest From Above'. His anthem 'Blessed be God the Father' is also well known. Whilst at Gloucester, Wesley made one last important contribution to church music, which was the publication of *The European Psalmist*, in 1872, containing many works of his own hymn and psalm tunes worked on during the previous twenty years.

Some Noteworthy Monuments in Gloucester Cathedral

Robert, Duke of Normandy

In the south ambulatory of Gloucester Cathedral stands the tomb of Robert of Normandy, who died in Cardiff Castle in 1134. Robert was the eldest son of William the Conqueror and was born in about 1054. He succeeded to his father's lands in

Normandy, whilst William Rufus was given England. Robert was in Italy on Crusade when Henry I succeeded to the English throne and Robert rushed back, attempting to invade England to claim the throne for himself. This action ended in failure and he was forced to renounce his claim to the

Robert, Duke of Normandy.

English throne. In return, Henry promised to make no claim on Robert's Norman lands and to pay him an annuity of 3,000 marks.

Henry, however, reneged on his promise, invaded Normandy and captured Robert at the Battle of Tinchebrai on 26 September 1106. Robert then spent the rest of his life as a prisoner at Cardiff Castle, where he died in February 1134. It is thought that he was buried in the chapter house.

Gloucester Cathedral's tomb, complete with its Irish Oak effigy of Robert, is a particularly interesting artefact from the thirteenth century. The tomb was painted during the reign of Charles II, but broken up during the Civil War and sold to Sir Humphrey Tracey of Stanway, Gloucestershire. It was returned to the cathedral following the Restoration. The effigy was repainted once more in 1791.

The most notable feature of the tomb is the effigy's crossed legs. It was thought to have symbolised someone who had participated in the Crusades; however, this theory is now not generally accepted. Throughout his life, Robert was nicknamed 'Curthose' because of the shortness of his legs. Perhaps the sculptor is trying to give Robert more vigour and show that his legs were perfectly fine after all. The effigy also depicts the thick stocking that surrounds the knight's knee and thigh. This was a medieval knight's way of avoiding being badly cut by their own armour if it was struck by an enemy.

The effigy rests upon a tomb that dates from around 1500. At the time of the Restoration, John Champion undertook repairs in roughly 1662. Robert chose to be buried at Gloucester Cathedral and he may well have been an early benefactor of the abbey.

Edward II

Edward II was born on 5 April 1284 at Caernarvon Castle and became the heir to the throne at 4 months old, when his elder brother died. He became the first English Prince of Wales on 7 February 1301 when he was 17 and, following the death of his father, Edward, he succeeded to the throne and was crowned at Westminster Abbey. His reign, however, is not generally regarded as being successful.

Edward II had favourites upon whom he often lavished extravagant gifts. These favourites were frequently unpopular with the barons – partly because Edward rewarded his favourites at the expense of the other barons and partly because he relied so heavily on their (often poor) advice. One such was Piers Gaveston, who was very close to Edward II during the early years of his reign. Indeed, contemporary chroniclers remarked on the two men's closeness and the 'love' shown between them. Edward lavished gifts on Gaveston, including a number of items of jewellery that had been given to Edward by his father, and this has led many historians to speculate that the king was homosexual. However, this is by no means certain, and Edward and Piers were both married at a time when their relationship was said to be particularly close. Edward married Isabella, the daughter of King Philip IV of France and Philip, known for being particularly homophobic, is unlikely to have allowed Isabella to marry Edward if there were credible suspicions for Edward's homosexuality. Furthermore, Edward went on to father four children (three were legitimate and one illegitimate).

In 1310, a group of barons rose up against Edward's poor rule and forced him to sign a number of 'ordinances' to govern England. The ordinances detailed forty-one different clauses and dealt with a wide range of issues. They restricted Edward's ability to go to war, held that Edward could only grant land with the agreement of the barons, and called for Gaveston to be exiled. Edward later persuaded the Pope to rescind the ordinances, which led to a long-running dispute with his barons. Edward refused to accept the exile of his favourite and, in 1312, Gaveston returned to England. On his return he was besieged at Scarborough Castle by a number of barons and, following the siege, he was captured and killed. Edward vowed revenge on the barons involved and was reportedly devastated by Gaveston's death.

Edward's next favourite, Hugh Despenser, was just as unpopular as Gaveston had been. The barons attacked Despenser's Welsh lands and, with the threat of civil war looming, Edward agreed to have Hugh banished. Then Edward went back on his word and arrested the ringleader, Henry of Lancaster, had him executed and brought Hugh back. It has been suggested that there was also a homosexual relationship between the king and Despenser, although this is difficult to prove.

Militarily, the reign of Edward II was unsuccessful. Edward's father had won control of Scotland by forcing the kings of Scotland to swear fealty to him, but the period was far from peaceful. Robert the Bruce, proclaiming his right to the Scottish throne, led a revolt and, as prince, Edward II was involved in a number of failed attempts to secure a decisive victory over the Scots. A new campaign to defeat Robert the Bruce resulted in a crushing defeat at the Battle of Bannockburn, on 24 June 1314. It has been regarded as one of the worst defeats in English history.

The tomb of Edward II. Note the recesses carved into the pillars to allow pilgrims access all the way around the tomb. (Author's collection)

Edward had married Isabella in 1308 when she was just 12 years old. The union was not a happy one, in part because of the close relationships that Edward forged with his favourites, particularly the Despensers. Eventually, Isabella took a lover of her own: Roger Mortimer. When Edward sent his wife to France in order to pay homage to her brother, the King of France, Isabella planned a rebellion. Alongside Mortimer she raised an army, helped by William, Count of Hainault, in return for a promise that Isabella's son (the future Edward III) would marry Hainault's daughter. On 24 September 1326, Isabella – who would earn the nickname 'the She-Wolf of France' – invaded England and was joined by many dissatisfied English nobles. Edward tried to make a stand against the advancing forces when they arrived outside London, but this was unsuccessful. He subsequently fled to Wales, where he was captured at Llantrisant on 16 November and taken prisoner to Kenilworth Castle. Parliament was summoned on 7 January 1327 and Edward was declared incapable of governing the country as he had allowed himself to be governed by others. He was accused of losing, through poor leadership, the kingdoms of Scotland, Ireland and Gascony; of becoming preoccupied with unsuitable occupations; and of losing the friendship of the King of France, amongst others. Edward II's position as king had become untenable and, on 25 January 1327, he was forced to abdicate in favour of his son.

In April of that year, Edward was moved to Berkeley Castle, Gloucestershire. From here, two unsuccessful attempts were made to release him and then his death was announced on 21 September 1327. Edward died in mysterious circumstances and precisely how he died remains unknown. The popularly accepted belief is that he died from having a red-hot

poker thrust up his anus and that his screams could be heard for miles around. However, contemporary accounts of Edward's death do not mention this but instead suggest strangulation or suffocation. Officially, Edward's death was put down to natural causes. It is not until the mid-1330s that the first mention of a red-hot poker appears.

The following month, Edward II's body arrived at St Peter's Abbey (now the cathedral) for public display. His burial took place there on 29 December 1327, although his heart was embalmed and sent to Isabella.

Edward III, his son and heir, arranged for the magnificent tomb of Edward II to be erected within the cathedral. It was installed in the 1330s, after the king was said to have become troubled by the part that he played in his father's downfall. The tomb is an early example of the English Court style and the alabaster effigy of the king's face – possibly made from a death mask – was the very first in England.

Edward III made several pilgrimages to visit his father's tomb and this tradition was continued by his sons: Edward, the Black Prince, and Richard II. Richard tried, unsuccessfully, to get Edward II canonised, as his grandfather had also been known for his piety throughout his reign and was particularly keen on expressing his devotion through the English saints: Thomas Becket and Edward the Confessor. The capitals of the tomb's columns are decorated with a white heart, which was the badge of Richard II and commemorates his stay when parliament was held in the city in 1378.

Edward II's tomb remained a popular pilgrimage site until the Reformation. The large number of visitor can be shown by the niches cut in the pillars surrounding the tomb. These were created to allow pilgrims to walk all the way around it. The architecture of the tomb may have gone some way towards influencing the style of the reminder of the cathedral and large parts of it were rebuilt with the money given by pilgrims visiting the shrine.

Dorothea Beale

A monument to Dorothea Beale, a head-mistress and education reformer, hangs in Gloucester Cathedral. She was born in London and was the fourth child to Miles Beale and Dorothea Margaret Complin. Miles Beale was a doctor and both parents encouraged their children's education, including that of their daughters. In 1848, the Governesses' Benevolent Institution founded Queen's College, Harley Street, where Dorothea received diplomas that certified her ability to teach many of the subjects that were studied by girls at the time. Within a year, she was her-self teaching mathematics at the college. Aged only 23, she accepted the post of headmistress at the preparatory school there.

In June 1858, Dorothea accepted the post of Principal of Cheltenham Ladies' College, a position that she retained until her death. At the time of her appointment, the college was faced with a number of problems: num-bers were falling, there was little money and the lease on the school buildings was due to expire in two years' time. Dorothea exer-cised the strictest economy and was able to reorganise the school's finances to ensure its survival. Initially, Beale had to face the preju-dices of the parents whose daughters attended the school. Parents did not want their daugh-ters to learn what they considered to be 'boy's subjects', such as science and mathematics; instead they were concerned that their daugh-ters should be educated to fulfil their domestic role successfully. Dorothea, who did much of

the teaching herself – especially in the early years – was gradually able to widen the syllabus. Mathematics was finally introduced in 1868.

Dorothea Beale's methods of teaching were highly successful and she regularly tested her pupils to ensure that the information had been learnt. Furthermore, she ensured from the outset that the girls would complete exter-nal examinations, which were often marked by Oxford dons. This guaranteed high stand-ards amongst her pupils and ensured that the school's success was known throughout the educational world. Unsurprisingly, under Dorothea's regime, pupil numbers rose steadily.

From the mid-1860s, Dorothea began to expound her views on the subject of wom-en's education. For example, on 19 April 1866 she gave evidence to the School's Enquiry Commission, known as the Taunton Commission, which published a report on the inadequacy of many girls' schools one year later. In October of that year, she also published an article in *Frazer* tackling the question of the medical fitness of girls to study and sit examinations in the same way as their male counterparts.

One of the main problems faced by girls' schools at the time was the lack of suit-ably qualified staff. Dorothea encouraged able pupils to enter the teaching profession by establishing a small boarding house for them. This later became St Hilda's College, Cheltenham. As well as providing many of the teachers for the college, she encour-aged these students to study for University of London degrees. Dorothea was also the founder of St Hilda's College, Oxford. It was her intention that this college would be for Cheltenham pupils or staff who wished to spend a year at Oxford, pursuing lei-surely study without necessarily taking any formal examinations. The scheme was strongly opposed by the heads of other women's colleges, who were concerned that it might adversely affect their efforts to allow women to take degrees. Nonetheless, St Hilda's Oxford was opened in 1893 and many of the students took the examinations.

More generally, Dorothea Beale helped to shape the future development of women's education. In 1874, she was one of eight founder members of the Association of Head Mistresses. At the time of her death, membership had grown to over 230. She also took part in numerous conferences and supported the Women's Suffrage movement. In 1902, she was awarded an LLD by Edinburgh University. Her successes at the Cheltenham Ladies' College are also evidenced by the large Gothic buildings that now form part of the school. Dorothea died on 9 November 1906 in Cheltenham. After a cremation in Birmingham, her ashes were interred, on 16 November, in Gloucester Cathedral during a ceremony that was attended by practically the entire Cheltenham Ladies' College.

Richard Pate

Richard Pate (1516–88) was a lawyer and the founder of Cheltenham Grammar School – which today is known as Pate's Grammar School, following its merger with Pate's Grammar School for Girls. His wealth, which seems to have been derived from former monastic lands, may have helped to advance his legal career and, in 1556, he became the Recorder of Gloucester.

As a founder of Cheltenham Grammar School, Pates stipulated detailed provisions for the number of scholars to be admitted and the standards that he expected them to meet. Prizes were to be given to the most outstanding pupils. Pates also made provision for a workhouse in Cheltenham, which he subjected to

an exacting criterion. The only people admitted to the house were over 60, had been born in the parish of Cheltenham and were incurably but not infectiously ill. Inmates were also required to be able to recite the Lord's Prayer and the Ten Commandments from memory.

Pate was responsible for the rebuilding of Matson House, on a site that had been owned by Llanthony Priory prior to the Dissolution. The house still stands (located opposite St Katherine's church, Matson) and is built in a style that is typical for the late sixteenth century in the Cotswolds. Matson House was also the location of Charles I's headquarters during his Siege of Gloucester in 1643 (*see* Gloucester and the Civil War p. 69).

Richard Pate died on 29 October 1588 and was buried in the south transept of Gloucester Cathedral, where a monument was erected depicting Pate in the dress of a lawyer of the period. The kneeling figures painted on the back of the tomb, showing Pate and his family, are now very faded and hardly discernable.

Thomas Machen

In the north aisle stands a monument to Thomas Machen, merchant of Gloucester, who was also the city's mayor. Machen was successful in business and politics and was part of the 'godly' faction in the Corporation. In 1566, he married Christine Baston (*c.* 1546–1615) and together they had thirteen children. Machen died on 18 October 1614 and this elaborate monument depicts Machen and his wife on either side of an arched recess, while in the middle stands a winged figure of time. Underneath, the couple's six sons and seven daughters are kneeling in prayer opposite each other. It is thought that Samuel Baldwin of Stroud may have created the monument, which retains much of its original paint.

Three

Historic Parish Churches, Religious Houses and Other Medieval Curiosities

Historic Parish Churches

St Mary de Lode Church

The church of St Mary de Lode is Saxon in origin and is regarded by many as being the oldest parish church in the city. The name originates from the Old English and refers to the ford, or lode, that crossed the River Severn close by. Over the years, the church has also been referred to as 'St Mary before the Gate of St Peter', 'St Mary Broadgate' and 'St Mary de Port'.

The church was built on an earlier Roman site and, during the rebuilding of the nave, in 1825–26, a Roman pavement was discovered. A trap door at the west end of the nave reveals the results of an excavation that took place in 1976–79 and includes part of a mosaic with alternating black and white panels. The archaeological dig showed that St Mary de Lode was built over two earlier Roman buildings: one dating from the second

to fourth centuries and one from the fifth to sixth centuries. The first Roman building was demolished to make way for the second: a Christian timber building. Burials were discovered which had been carried out in a Christian manner and so the building may have been a church or a mausoleum. A portion of the mosaic is on display in the nave.

The present church consists of a twelfth- and thirteenth-century tower and chancel with a nave erected in an impoverished early Gothic revival. The nave was rebuilt by James Cooke, a Gloucester mason, in 1825–26 and is supported by octagonal stone piers with cast-iron cores in an effect which is somewhat odd but still attractive. The nave arch is Norman and has been described as 'appearing like the entrance to a tunnel'. The chancel is also late twelfth century and was extended eastwards, with the addition of a chancel arch, during the thirteenth century. The chancel is also home to a recumbent effigy of a priest in Eucharistic vestments. It is possibly William de Chamberlayne (d. 1304) or John de Rodberrow (d. 1302). In the nave, the pulpit dates from the fifteenth century and, on one of its panels, a Tudor rose has been carved.

On the north wall, there is a tablet in memory of Malcolm Cotton-Brown, the eldest son of a well-known American family, whose plane crashed at Brockworth.

St Mary de Lode church.

After attending the military engineering camp of the Massachusetts Institute of Technology in the summer of 1917, Cotton-Brown made an application to join the Royal Flying Corps, which had recently opened a branch in Canada to help with recruitment for the war effort.

Following instruction at the Canadian school, Port Worth, Texas, Cotton-Brown then sailed for England to complete his training, after which he became a lieutenant in the Royal Flying Corps and joined No. 90 Squadron. The squadron did not see overseas service and Malcolm Cotton-Brown was killed near Brockworth, when he flew a defective plane on 23 July 1917.

In the south wall of the naves, two stained-glass windows, mostly heraldic, were installed in the year 2000. Created by Roy Coomber, one is dedicated to the poet Ivor Gurney, the other to Captain Robert Laurence Nairac (1945–77). Nairac joined the army whilst he was studying at Oxford and was commissioned into the Grenadier Guards before being sent to Belfast in 1973. On 14/15 May 1977, Nairac was murdered by the IRA and his body has never been recovered. In February 1979, it was announced that Nairac was to be posthumously awarded a George Cross, the highest honour for gallantry.

St Mary de Lode church is also home to an historic organ. The fine mahogany case of the organ dates from around 1760–80 and some of the stopped wooden flute pipes have the date 1766 inscribed on their pipes. The organ came from the nearby St Nicholas' church, after it was made redundant in 1968. The instrument originally consisted of a single manual (keyboard) and, according to tradition, the organ was formerly at Moorfields and may, therefore, have been played by Handel.

St Mary de Crypt

This church is Norman in origin and was first recorded from the 1140s. The cruciform plan of the structure, together with its central tower, is an indication of its Norman beginning, although the billeted hoodmould of the west doorway is all that remains of the original building. The west doorway also has a tympanum depicting the *Agnus Dei* (Lamb of God), which was created by S.W. Daukes and J.R. Hamilton in 1845–46. In 1241, the church came under the control of Llanthony Priory and was later added to during the Perpendicular period. It was traditionally thought that much of this work could be attributed to Henry Dene, Prior of Llanthony Priory, 1467–1501. However, it is now thought that the Perpendicular work is earlier, since the church was described as new in 1401.

The medieval interest does not end there, however. Inside the chancel, wall paintings, though sadly incomplete, date from roughly 1530. On the north wall, the paintings show the Adoration of the Magi, whilst on the south side, a few details of what was probably a Marian subject survive. These surviving paintings are considered some of the finest of the period.

A blocked doorway on the north exterior wall gave access to the crypts from which the church's name is derived. Those beneath the nave were used as a tavern during the sixteenth and seventeenth centuries. Later the crypt was used as a store, until the 1840s restoration by S.W. Daukes and J.R. Hamilton.

The pulpit in the nave dates from approximately 1600 and it is where George Whitefield preached his first sermon, in 1736. The nave altar uses a seventeenth-century Communion table from St John the Baptist's church, Northgate Street, which was placed here during a reordering that took place in the 1970s. St Mary de Crypt church also possesses two parish chests: one chest, dating from 1603, is intricately carved and includes a scene of the Annunciation; the other, which is plainer and probably older, also came from St John the Baptist's church.

The church contains a number of interesting monuments. The south chapel holds a tomb chest of Sir Thomas (d. 1566) and Lady Bell (d. 1567). The tomb of Dorothy Snell (d. 1746), crafted by Peter Scheemakers, is a particularly fine monument and shows a seated female reading a book with a cornucopia at her feet. A head and shoulders sculpture of Dorothy Snell is carved on to an oval, where a weeping putto stands. The south

chapel also contains Robert Raikes's memorial (*see* Robert Raikes p. 79). In the north chapel are the brasses of John and Joan Cooke, who founded the Crypt Grammar School (*see* St Mary de Crypt Grammar School p. 66). In the chancel lies the grave of James Wood (d. 1836), a well-known eccentric Gloucester banker, who was famed for his miserliness and is said to have inspired Charles Dickens's character of Ebenezer Scrooge. His grave is noticeably more worn than the other memorials in the chancel of similar vintage, suggesting that it was constructed of inferior stone – a reflection on the miserliness of the man himself, perhaps? In reality, following his death, Wood's estate was largely consumed by legal wrangling over a disputed codicil (*see* James 'Jemmy' Wood p. 88).

Billeted hoodmould with tympanum, dating from the restoration of 1845–46, by S.W. Daukes and J.R. Hamilton.

St Michael's Tower and Rudhall's Bell Foundry

Standing at The Cross, this substantial west tower, believed to be constructed between 1460–70, is all that is left of a medieval church that once stretched a further 80ft (24m) to the east. The nave and the chancel, which dated from the twelfth century, were taken down and rebuilt by Fulljames and Waller a little further to the south in 1849–51 to permit the widening of the road. The church was demolished in 1955 after being shut in 1940, and the parish church was united with St Mary de Crypt.

A 'common' or 'curfew bell' was tolled daily at 4 a.m. and 6 p.m. The evening bell continued to be rung until the outbreak of the Second World War; save for a gap between 1854–72 when the peal was silent. In 1956 the ten bells were taken down, two were given to the cathedral and the rest sold. In subsequent years the tower was used as a bell-ringing museum and later as a tourist information office.

St Michael's Tower.

The tower is, at the time of writing, administered by the Gloucester Civic Trust and bells continue to play an important role in telling the history of St Michel's tower. A curfew bell from All Saint's, High Wycombe, was installed in the tower in 2012. In addition, two more bells from the pre-2012 ring of St Michael's church, Stone, Staffs, have been placed on display. These two bells were cast by Abraham Rudall, a Gloucester bell founder, in 1710.

A blue plaque on the side of the post office, in The Oxbode, gives the location of the former bell foundry that cast so many of the county's bells. The foundry was started by Abraham Rudall the Elder (1657–1736). His name first appears in the accounts of St Mary de Crypt from 1677, where he may have been assisting the bell founders William Coey and Richard Purdue III. The earliest known ring of bells, cast by Rudhall, are located at St Nicholas' church, Oddington, Gloucestershire, which date from 1684. Rudhall's bells were well-regarded in their own time because of their excellent musical qualities. In 1691, Rudhall was made a freeman of the city and joined the College Youths' Society of Bellringers at Bath in 1699. He retired in 1718 and his son, Abraham Rudhall the Younger (1680–1735), took over the family business. The elder Rudhall died on 25 January 1736 and was buried in Gloucester Cathedral. Upon Abraham Rudhall the Younger's death the previous year, the business had passed to Abel Rudhall (1714–51). Three of Abel Rudhall's sons carried on the trade: Thomas Rudhall (1740?–83),

Charles Rudhall (1746–1815) and John Rudhall (1760–1835). John was the last bell founder to bear the Rudhall name. The foundry at Gloucester was nominally closed in 1828 but there are bells that bear John Rudhall's name dating from 1835.

St Nicholas' Church

The first mention of St Nicholas' church comes from a charter of about 1180 where Sigar the priest is noted. By 1203 the church was known as St Nicholas of the Bridge of Gloucester; it is thought to have been a royal foundation and therefore belonged to the Crown. The building's location and orientation give clues about the church's origins. Constructed outside a Saxon burgh, a number of buildings were probably cleared to accommodate it, which would explain its cramped situation. The churchyard also fits exactly into a burgage plot that would have been laid out by the Saxons. A burgage plot was a characteristic of many medieval towns in which the house (or shop front) stands at the front of a long strip of land, laid out at right angles to the street alignment. St Nicholas' church follows an east-to-west alignment, a common feature of later Norman churches.

The church was built close to the River Severn and is located on a main thoroughfare. Bridges over rivers were seen, in the Middle Ages, as holy places. Travellers across the bridge would often gave alms to churches located near to them and these churches would generally be given the responsibility of maintaining the bridge. This was a function that St Nicholas' may have provided, especially when it was given control of St Bartholomew's Hospital that stood by the bridge (*see* St Bartholomew's Hospital p. 49).

The patron saint of the church, St Nicholas, became popular in the Middle Ages, when his relics were moved from Myra in Turkey to Bari in southern Italy, in 1087. St Nicholas was also the patron saint of sailors and this choice of patron may have been influenced by the church's close proximity to the quay on the River Severn.

The original Norman church consisted of a nave, north aisle and a chancel. The church underwent a series of rebuilds over the years to emerge as one of the city's largest and wealthiest medieval churches. Of the twelfth-century church, three piers measuring 3ft 6in in diameter, plus two arches of the nave arcade survive. In addition, a carved tympanum of the *Agnus Dei* (Lamb of God) survives, located above the south door. In 1347, a south-west porch was added to the nave and a decorated style of window was inserted into the south wall of the nave. The fourteenth century bought a new style to the church and a window at the east end of the south aisle was replaced with one in the Perpendicular style. In the fifteenth century, the east window and south-aisle windows were replaced, again in the Perpendicular style.

In the north transept, the south wall of the south aisle contains piscinas, indicating the presence of chantry chapels. A piscina was a basin for washing vessels associated with the Mass, set in or against the wall on the south side of the altar. Chantry chapels were found inside a church for the celebration of Masses, principally dedicated to the soul of the founder. In the south wall of the chancel, a piscina with credence (a shelf within or beside the piscina) was provided for the high altar. Another later addition, in the sixteenth century, was the provision of squints in the north and south walls. These provided a view of the Mass being celebrated at the high altar.

St Nicholas' church.

Bracket clock on St Nicholas' church tower.

The church tower dates from the fifteenth century. It measures 23ft (7m) square, is formed of three stages and is 90ft (27m) high, topped by a truncated spire. From the ground, the tower has a noticeable lean. It is, in fact, 2ft 6in (0.7cm) from perpendicular, owing to the fact that the tower is built on marshy ground. The spire was also damaged during the Siege of Gloucester in 1643. In 1783, John Bryan truncated the spire as the tower was so much out of alignment. He replaced the top with a coronet, pinnacles and ball-finals that can be seen today. In 1925–26, the tower was strengthened and 30 tons of concrete are said to have been pumped in to strengthen the foundations. On the side of the tower a bracket clock, dating from 1716, is a well-known local landmark. For many years, St Nicholas' church was a Corporation church and there are several fine monuments of aldermen and other city officials. These include a chest tomb with the effigy of Alderman John Walton (d. 1613) and his wife (d. 1626), and the wall tablet of Revd Richard Green

(d. 1711) with Corinthian columns and broken segmental pediment.

On the west wall of the south aisle, a section of a gallery front has been erected. The panelling is Jacobean and dates from around 1621. The gallery once extended across the width of the nave but was removed during the church's restoration by John Jacques in 1865. A blocked opening above the south-west porch may indicate where the stairs to the gallery used to go. Jacques was also responsible for many of the interior church furnishings, including the pulpit and the pews.

The main south door had attached a 'sanctuary knocker', now found in the city museum. It depicted the head and part of the body of a demon, with long hair, ears and hairy forelegs. The demon carried the head of an old woman on its back and had a large ring in its mouth. This curiosity dates from the fourteenth century and was apparently used by offenders seeking sanctuary in the church. The depiction of a demon may be a pun on the dedication of the church. A popular name for the devil was 'Old Nick'.

St John's Methodist Church

Previously known as St John the Baptists church, St John's church, with its classical façade, dates from 1732–34, when the church was rebuilt by Edward and Thomas Woodward of Chipping Camden. The tower (just out of sight in the image below) is older, dating from the mid-fifteenth century, and is built in the Perpendicular style. The ribbed spire was truncated in 1910 by H.A. Dancey, who replaced the top with a ball finial. Inside, an oak reredos dates from 1734. The choir stalls are much later, inserted by Waller, Son & Wood in 1882, and they project into the nave in typical Waller style. The pulpit of St John's was once a triple-decker, which was reduced to one tier, probably during the church's restoration by Waller. The Methodist preachers John Wesley and George Whitefield are both known to have preached from it, in 1739 and 1741 respectively. Following the sale of the nearby Methodist place of worship, the Methodist congregation shared St John's with the Anglican congregation. This arrangement lasted until 1994, when the Anglicans had no further use for the building. Since then, the church has been in the sole charge of the Methodists. This building was also where Revd Thomas Stock served as rector and a memorial tablet to Stock can be found in the nave.

St John's Methodist church in Northgate Street.

Religious Houses of Gloucester

St Oswald's Priory

Shortly before 900, Ethelfleda of Mercia, daughter of King Alfred, founded a Saxon minster. The minster's dedication to Oswald refers to a seventh-century Saxon King of Northumbria, whose bones were translated here in 909, following a raid into Viking territory. Consequently, the priory became a major pilgrimage centre and Ethelfleda, along with her husband, King Ethelred, would later be buried here. In 1152–53 the priory became a house of Augustinian canons and, after the Dissolution, the north aisle and transept was used as the parish church of St Catherine. The remainder of the priory was allowed to fall into ruins until, following damage caused during the Siege of Gloucester in 1643, a partial demolition took place in 1655–56.

When Edwin seized the kingdom of Northumbria in 616, St Oswald was forced to flee to Scotland and became a Christian at Iona. On Edwin's death, in 633, he returned to Northumbria. Despite having a smaller army, he defeated Cadwalla, who had been tyrannically ruling Northumbria during the previous year, in a battle for the throne that took place at Havenfelt, near Hexham. Before the battle it is recorded that St Oswald set up a wooden cross to pray. Following the victory he worked alongside St Aiden, who was given the island of Lindisfarne as an episcopal seat. The pair travelled across the kingdom on a number of missionary journeys and St Oswald translated St Aiden's sermons. Consequently, these sermons met with a considerable degree of success and a significant number of conversions. Oswald's reign lasted eight years until he was defeated by the pagan king, Penda of Mercia, at the Battle of Maserfield, Salop.

The surviving ruins of the Saxon minster principally consist of a long north wall. It is pierced by a Norman arcade, dating from the mid-twelfth century, which was inserted when the church was enlarged to include a north aisle. The remains of the arch from the north aisle to the north transept can also be seen. A number of Saxon crosses have been discovered at the site and are now in the care of the city museum.

A short distance away, to the north, polychromatic brick gate piers belong to a new St Catherine's church, constructed by Medland, Maberly & Medland, which was built in 1867–68. This church was demolished, in 1921, having been replaced by a church designed by Walter B. Wood, in London Road, Wotton.

Llanthony Priory

Llanthony Priory, Llanthony Road, is today surrounded by industrial development. In the Middle Ages, the priory was the richest Augustinian house in the kingdom. Llanthony Priory was not, however, the first priory to bear that name. The first Llanthony Priory (Llanthony Prima) was founded in around 1120 in the Black Mountains, Monmouthshire. However, following the death of Henry I in 1136, the priory became caught up in a Welsh rebellion and was severely damaged. In the same year, Miles of Hereford founded Llanthony Secunda at Gloucester for the fugitive Augustinian canons.

Developments after 1100 led to a large number of Augustinian houses being established in Britain. Such patronage was

The remains of Llanthony Priory's outer gatehouse, dating from the sixteenth century.

promoted by the archbishop, as well as Henry I and his wife, Queen Matilda. The introduction of canons (who could be thought of as 'clerical monks') to look after a parish was one way that bishops could exercise effective control over the churches in their diocese by taking control of patronage, at least, away from the laity. All Augustinian houses followed the rule of St Augustine, which was often chosen because of its adaptability to the circumstances of the house. It could be used by those religious communities who sought to lead a more contemplative life, or by groups of hermits who decided to live together, as was the case when Llanthony Prima was founded.

Llanthony Secunda went on to become a very wealthy priory, well known for its hospitality. The priory, with its close proximity to the royal castle of Gloucester, also enjoyed a number of royal visitors: Henry III stayed in 1242, Edward II in 1327, and Queen Eleanor – who stayed whilst she lived at Gloucester Castle during the year of 1277 – was given permission to walk in the priory garden. A visit by the first Tudor king, Henry VII, in 1501, bestowed the archbishopric of Canterbury on Henry Dene, the prior. It is perhaps not surprising, therefore, that when the church was rebuilt between 1493 and 1513, it was the wealthiest Augustinian house in England.

Llanthony Priory.

Today, nothing remains of the church, which is thought to have had two west towers, or the cloistral buildings. The boundary wall at the eastern end of the site probably cuts through where the west end of the church once stood. Only fragments of the inner and outer courts of this once great Augustinian priory now remain.

Alongside Llanthony Road, part of the outer gatehouse still stands, dating from around 1500. The pedestrian archway has a small window, with a hoodmold above it, and around the window are three shields. The shield above the window carry the royal arts, on the right of the window are the arms of Prior Dene and to the left of the window are the arms of de Bohun. The de Bohuns were descendants of Miles and ten generations of this family were buried within the church or chapter house. In addition, a fragment of the vehicle arch can be seen to the north of the pedestrian entrance.

Evidence of the priory's wealth can be seen in the stretch of the battlemented precinct wall further south. The wall was rebuilt in brick during the sixteenth century and consists of some noteworthy patterning, some chequerwork, a pattern of four lozenges and a wayside cross. It is one of the oldest brick-built structures in Gloucestershire.

Inside the priory grounds is the only currently roofed building. It formed part of the grange that ran between the inner and outer courts, and is a complex building, dating from many different time periods. The farmhouse at the south end was built in around 1855–69, possibly by PC Hardwick. The adjoining six-bay stable consists of a thirteenth-century stone ground floor, with several Tudor-arched mullioned windows. Many of these were reset in the seventeenth or eighteenth century. The upper storey of timber framing was added in about 1500.

To the north of the farmhouse are the remains of a large fifteenth-century barn. Also of note is the ruined south range, where the thick stone walls have been faced in brick, both inside and out. Small Tudor-arched windows are also in evidence. The south range was probably altered in the seventeenth or eighteenth century when the floor level was raised and the easternmost part sectioned off to be used as a coach house.

The Coming of the Friars to Gloucester

From the 1230s, a radically new form of monasticism swept through Britain. The friars were not like the Benedictine monks, who led their lives from within the cloister, with the monastery financially supported by the ownership of land. The friars chose, in imitation of the apostles, to beg for their livelihood as they wandered from place to place. Gloucester was no exception to this new religious expression and three houses of friars were established: the Dominicans, the Franciscans and the Carmelites, or Whitefriars. The buildings associated with the Carmelite Friars were mostly taken down shortly after the Reformation and no trace of the buildings is evident today. The present name of the site, 'Friars Ground', is the only clue of the area's past. More substantive remains of the Dominican and Franciscan houses remain and these are detailed overleaf.

Blackfriars

Blackfriars, off Ladybellegate Street, was home to the order of Friars Preachers, otherwise known as the Dominican order after their founder, St Dominic; or as the 'Black Friars', named after the colour of their habit. Blackfriars is one of only three Dominican friaries to have survived with a large degree of completeness. (The others are at Norwich and Newcastle-upon-Tyne.)

St Dominic (c. 1171–1221) was an Augustinian canon who, in 1204, began to undertake missions against the perceived Cathar heresy in the Montpellier region of southern France. From his experience of trying to combat this heresy, by argument and persuasion, Dominic likely conceived the idea of forming a group of poor men dedicated to following in his footsteps. Dominic established the Friars Preachers in 1215, in Toulouse. Papal support for Dominic's order was received and, in 1217, Dominic sent his companions away from their Toulouse head-quarters to go on peripatetic missions.

In 1221, a group of Friars Preachers, led by Gilbert de Fresney, came to England. Gilbert was presented to Archbishop Stephen Langton of Canterbury, who called for Gilbert to preach a sermon. Gilbert's sermon must have made a great impression on Stephen Langton as he gave the friars his enthusiastic support. The friars then made their way to Oxford, the country's fore-most seat of learning. The choice indicates the main precepts of the order and mem-bers were expected to be devoted to study as well as prayer. Study of theology would bear fruit in the world by communication of the Word of God, that is, the knowledge of Christ's salvation contained within the Bible. Certainly the education and learning of the friars helped to bridge a need within the medieval Church. The Friars Preachers, with their education and training, stood in marked contrast to a great number of secular clergy, who lacked any regimented learning.

Another enthusiastic supporter was Henry III (1207–72), who supported a number of Blackfriars' establishments, including the house at Gloucester. This house, established in 1239 by Sir Stephen de Hermshall, was located on a site just inside the city's walls. Henry III provided the timber for the roofs of the friary and building continued until around 1270. At this point, the friary would have been home to between thirty and forty friars. The church, consecrated in 1274, was altered substantially in the fourteenth century, with vaulting add to the south aisle and crossing, and the widening of the north aisle.

In 1539, following the Reformation, the buildings were sold to Alderman Thomas Bell, a capper and cloth maker. Bell set about converting the friary buildings into a mansion house, known as Bell's Place. In doing so, Bell shortened the church, especially truncating the nave and a smaller section of the chan-cel. After the death of Thomas Bell (d. 1566) and his wife Joan (d. 1567), Blackfriars passed into the hands of the Dennis family. During the eighteenth century, up until the early twentieth century, Blackfriars was converted for a number of industrial uses, including a stonemason's workshop.

The Ministry of Works acquired the site in the 1960s and renovation began. The resto-ration works revealed much of the original thirteenth-century fabric and Blackfriars is now in the care of English Heritage.

The surviving friary church is typical of many contemporary examples and consists of a large nave, enabling a large number of laity to be accommodated in order to hear the friar's sermons. The chancel is much narrower in order to accommodate the friars. Differences in the construction of the walls of the church indicate where the rebuilding by Thomas Bell took place; the original thirteenth-century church was constructed from limestone rubble with ashier dressings, while Bell's alterations used coursed ashlar. Twentieth-century restoration has removed all the post-medieval floors to recreate the interior space of the original building. The thirteenth-century scissor-brace timber roof survives over the majority of the nave and the chancel, the latter of which houses a fine sixteenth-century chimneypiece. Its construction owes to the fact that the chancel became Bell's Great Hall.

The cloister to the south of the church was 80ft (24.4m) square and it is the south range that remains the most intact. The ground floor, with its low roof, was probably used for storage, while the upper floor contains a scriptorium or library – a rare survival. This scriptorium contains twenty-nine medieval study carrels, lit by small windows, and is separated by short stone screen walls with segmentally moulded arched heads.

Greyfriars

The friary church ruins are all that remain of the Franciscan friary that was founded by Thomas Lord Berkeley in about 1231. The Franciscans take their name from the founder of their order, St Francis of Assisi (1181–1226), and are also known as the Friars Minor, or as the Greyfriars – this name being derived from the simple habit that they wore.

St Francis was the son of a wealthy cloth merchant of Assisi, who underwent a dramatic conversion. One day, it is said that St Francis heard a voice telling him to 'go and repair my house which you see is falling down'. Consequently, Francis sold some of his father's cloth in order to repair the semi-derelict church of San Damiano, near Assisi. This led to a prolonged conflict with his father and ultimately caused Francis to renounce his father's inheritance and embrace absolute poverty. The Bishop of Assisi gave Francis new clothes in order that Francis might begin his new role as a mendicant. Within a few years, Francis had gathered some followers around him and composed a simple rule by which to live, following in the footsteps of Christ. Crucially, for the order to survive, he had also received papal approval. In 1217, the Friars Minor sent their first members across the Alps to live in poverty, beg for food and shelter, and to preach the Gospel to all.

The coming of the friars to Britain is well documented for, in 1258/59, Thomas of Eccleston, an English Franciscan, wrote *De Adventu Fratrum Minorum in Anglium (On the Coming of the Friars Minor to England)*. It was the Benedictine monks of Fécamp Monastery who arranged passage to England for a group of nine friars. Led by Agnellus of Pisa, they landed at Dover on 10 September 1224 and proceeded straight to Canterbury. The friars would eventually split into two groups, with five remaining in a newly established school for their use and the other four travelling to London where they rented a room for a short time with the Dominicans. This pattern of foundation was repeated again when Richard of Ingeworth and Richard of Devon left shortly afterwards for Oxford. They, again, stayed with the Dominicans until they were able to rent a house in the parish of St Ebbe.

Greyfriars Friary.

The Franciscans were able to establish themselves more quickly in Britain than the Dominican friars, as they were willing to start a new friary with only a handful of brethren and rely on rapid recruitment to make up the numbers. The Dominicans, by contrast, were insistent on having a full complement of thirteen brethren before establishing a new site.

The ruins at Gloucester principally consist of the nave of the friary church. This dates from 1516, when the church was rebuilt. The nave – wide enough to allow a large body of laity to be accommodated to hear sermons by the friars – was nearly of equal width to the north aisle. This is a unique feature amongst English mendicant churches, although a number of friars' churches in Germany also share this attribute.

The remainder of the friary has been lost to later development, including Greyfriars House,

built in 1810, at the westernmost part of the nave, and the Eastgate Market Hall. Immediately after the surrender of the friary to Henry VIII, in 1538, the site was converted into a brew house – a purpose for which it was ideally suited, given that the friary was supplied with a piped-water supply from Robinswood Hill. By the eighteenth century, several dwellings were erected within the shell of the friary. During the Siege of Gloucester, in 1643, Greyfriars was severely damaged by artillery fire and evidence of this abounds in the surviving walls. During 1975–77, conservation work was undertaken by H. Gordon Slade, the Ancient Monuments Area Architect. During this time, two facsimile armorial shields, of Chandos and Clifford of Frampton, were inserted on to the external nave south wall; the stone originals were possibly from a former funerary monument.

Medieval Hospitals

London Road: St Margaret's Hospital and St Mary Magdalene's Hospital

Heading out of Gloucester on the London Road, one encounters two leper hospitals, both founded in the early twelfth century. One of these hospitals, St Margaret's, was administered by St Peter's Abbey and dedicated to St Margaret of Scotland and St Sepulchre. The only surviving part of this medieval hospital is the chapel, which dates from the early fourteenth century. Surviving charters show that, during the Middle Ages, the hospital contained a governor, a prior, brethren and sisters, and a chaplain. Sometimes provision was made for the hospital for a nominal rent; for example, John del Hoke let land at Hucclecote to the hospital for an annual payment of a root of ginger.

Cases of leprosy declined sharply in the sixteenth century throughout Europe. Samuel Rudder, a Gloucestershire historian writing in the 1770s, notes the decline of the disease in Ireland, where their English rulers under Cromwell had limited the 'people's living so such upon salmon and other fish, which every river and brook abounded with, and the poor people had for catching'. Other plants and vegetables were introduced into people's diets and consequently, because of the reduced consumption of fish, leprosy cases declined and many leper hospitals were now 'gone to ruin'. Gloucester's leper hospitals became almshouses for those too infirm to work. In 1862, the old buildings, excepting the chapel, were demolished and the picturesque

United Hospital was built. The building, designed by F.S. Waller, consists of patterned brickwork with Gothic details. Today, the site is known simply as St Margaret's.

Approximately 0.25 miles further northeast lies the leper hospital of St Mary Magdalene. Only part of the chapel here survives. The hospital was founded by Walter, Constable of Gloucester Castle, in the early twelfth century, with an endowment of £12 6s 8d per annum to pay for two loaves of bread daily for distribution amongst the inmates. The hospital was administered by Llanthony Priory and, following the decline of leprosy, it became an almshouse. In 1617,

James I gave £13 per annum to assist with the support of nineteen inmates, on the condition that the hospital was renamed 'King James' Hospital'. In 1636, statutes show that the hospital provided for ten men and nine women. In the long term, finances at the hospital were never secure and by the 1830s parts of the hospital were in a ruinous condition. The hospital became united with St Margaret's in 1861, when a new almshouse was constructed.

The surviving part of the chapel dates from the early twelfth century. When the nave was demolished in 1861, the Norman south doorway was reset into the chancel

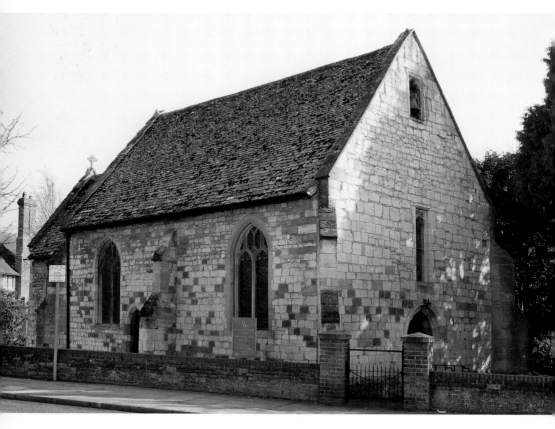

The surviving part of St Margaret's Hospital.

The surviving part of St Mary Magdalene's Hospital.

arch facing east. Its surround is highly deco-rated, with spiral shafts with pellets, capitals with beaded interlace and an arch with two orders of chevron. To the left of the entrance there is medieval graffiti on the wall of the chapel, presumably left by pilgrims. There are symbols for All Saints Day, Holy Cross Day, an Epiphany Star, the knot of St Valentine and a fleur-de-lis of the Blessed Virgin Mary.

Inside the chapel, a recumbent effigy of a lady (c. 1290) is thought to have been brought from St Kyneburgh's Chapel, which once stood near the Southgate. Local legend suggests that this effigy is of St Kyneburgh herself, a princess who fled to Gloucester to escape a marriage. She took up employ-ment as a baker's servant but his wife grew

jealous and Kyneburgh was murdered and thrown into a well. When her body was discovered, she was buried nearby and miracles were soon reported by those who sought her intercession. However, it is more likely that the effigy depicts a member of the de Bohun family, who patronised St Kyneburgh's chapel in the thirteenth and fourteenth centuries.

St Bartholomew's Hospital

St Bartholomew's Hospital stands marooned in the centre of a busy traffic gyratory system. The origins of the hospital can be traced back to the twelfth-century reign of Henry II and the building of a bridge across the River Severn. William Myparty built a house to accommodate the labourers constructing

St Bartholomew's Hospital.

the bridge and, following completion of the project, he gave the building as a hospital for the sick and dying, and as a resting place for travellers. In 1229, the hospital was given to St Nicholas' church, which levied tolls on the bridge. In medieval times, the Church was often given the charge of important infrastructure, such as bridges, as they were one of the few long-lasting institutions in medieval society.

The hospital suffered from mixed fortunes. During the thirteenth century, due to the depredations caused by the Barons' War, the bridge and the hospital were left in a ruinous state and the king was petitioned to fund the repairs. In 1401, the hospital was exempted from taxation owing to the lack of funds at the institution. However, by the sixteenth century, St Bartholomew's Hospital was the largest and richest of the three ancient hospitals in Gloucester. Deriving its income from several endowments, St Bartholomew's was able to support six priests and a master, and had thirty-two inmates.

In 1564, the hospital was conveyed to the Corporation to look after the forty people who lived there and the accommodation was rebuilt and improved. By 1636, statutes show that the hospital was caring for twenty men and thirty women, who were entitled to a weekly allowance of 2s 6d. At this time, the hospital supported a community that included a physician, a surgeon, a porter, a beadle and a minister of religion who provided services in the hospital chapel and gave spiritual guidance to the people living there.

Despite a number of endowments to the hospital over the years, the building was allowed to fall into a ruinous condition once more. In 1789, the old buildings were demolished and replaced by a new hospital designed by local architect William Price in the then fashionable Gothic style. The building consists of a long south-facing ashlar front and embattled parapet. A small central porch gave access to a (now blocked) lobby, which then led to a spacious hallway, with staircase, and from there to the former chapel. The brick semi-circular apse of the chapel projects out from the north of the building. The building used to possess a small bell tower and numerous chimneystacks; however, these were taken down in roughly 1966.

After construction, the Bishop of Gloucester consecrated the new chapel on 1 October 1790. In 1890, St Bartholomew's Hospital became part of the United Hospitals, which included Gloucester's two other ancient hospitals: St Mary Magdalene and St Margaret, both located in London Road (*see* St Mary Magdalene's Hospital and St Margaret's Hospital p. 47). A sale of the site by the municipal charity trustees led to the restoration of the building during the 1980s, which now forms part of a shopping centre.

Other Medieval Curiosities

Our Lady's Well

The footpath leading north through the churchyard of St Swithun's church, Hempsted, leads (after about quarter of a mile) to a holy well, dedicated to the Blessed Virgin Mary. The well is surrounded by a small rectangular well-house, with thick stone slabs forming the roof, which dates from the late fourteenth century. The ogee-headed entrance is at the west of the structure, whilst a much-weathered carving, beneath the east gable, is thought to depict the Blessed Virgin and St Anne with an angel. The spot has fine views west across the River Severn towards Highnam and May Hill.

The King's Board

The King's Board is located in Hillfield Gardens, London Road, although it originally stood in the middle of Westgate Street. According to local tradition, the King's Board was given to Gloucester by Richard II (1367–99). Certainly, the architecture of the structure would suggest that it dates from the late fourteenth century. One theory is that, because of its small size, its original function was to provide a preaching cross for use by friars and the carvings in the spandrels could well be scenes from Christ's ministry. By 1580, however, it was in use as a butter market. In 1693, its roof, which was surmounted by a cross, was taken down in order to

The King's Board.

Detail of carving: this one shows Christ's entry into Jerusalem on a donkey.

accommodate a water cistern to store water pumped up from the Severn.

The King's Board has moved a few times during its history. In 1750 it was taken down during improvement works to the city and re-erected in the ornamental garden of Gloucester Castle, owned by the Hyett family. During 1780, a new jail was built on the castle site and the Board moved to a house in Barton Street. It was relocated again, during the mid-nineteenth century, to Tibberton Court, the home of W.P. Price, chairman of the Midland Railway Company. Finally, in 1937, the King's Board was returned to the city and re-erected in its present location, Hillfield Gardens.

Four

Inns and Public Houses

The New Inn

THE NEW INN, Northgate Street is a fine example of a medieval coaching inn. It was built in about 1450 to accommodate the many pilgrims to St Peter's Abbey visiting the shrine of Edward II. Traditionally, the building of the New Inn has been ascribed to a monk: John de Twyning.

In 1553, a proclamation was read from the inn's gallery, declaring Lady Jane Grey to be the new monarch following the death of Edward VI. Gloucester was one of only three places that announced the reign of the nine-day queen. Later that same year, the inn was host to knights, yeomen and gentlemen to celebrate the ascension of Mary Tudor to the throne.

The gallery's courtyard would have been the setting for entertainments and plays. Of particular interest is the carved, but now headless, angel on the southern corner of the building, adjacent to the lane. In the courtyard, a nineteenth-century sculpture depicts a lion fighting a serpent and symbolises the triumph of good over evil.

The New Inn, Northgate Street.

The courtyard at the New Inn.

In 1896, C.S. Rolls, the co-founder of Rolls-Royce, had an enforced stay at the inn after his car broke down. Rolls had been driving his Peugeot down the steep Birdlip Hill when his brakes failed. Shaken by the incident, he stopped over at the New Inn whilst repairs were made to his car. The following morning, Rolls started the car using the starting handle but, having been left in gear, it leapt forward and Rolls was run over by his own car. Rolls was unhurt by the accident but the car also ran into a cart, which he had to repair before he could continue his journey.

The Fleece Hotel

The Fleece Hotel, Westgate Street, was built in around 1500 for pilgrims visiting the abbey. The church retained ownership of the building until 1799. Its best-known feature is the twelfth-century undercroft – probably part of a merchant's store – over which the inn was built.

Nos 43–45 Westgate Street

Nos 43 and 45 Westgate were once two sep-
arate properties dating from the sixteenth
century. No. 43 Westgate Street was known
as the Union Inn until, in 1990, the two
properties were joined to create an enlarged
pub. No. 45 Westgate Street had been given
a new façade in the eighteenth century and,
looking closely at the upper storeys, it is possible to see that a number of windows are
false. This occurs where the façade projects
beyond the gable end of the building.

In the nineteenth century, the building was owned by John Pritchard, a tailor,
who is thought to have been the inspiration
behind Beatrix Potter's *The Tailor of Gloucester*.
Pritchard had been working on a waistcoat on
Friday, which was unfinished at the close of the
day. When he returned, on Monday morning, he found the waistcoat completed, save
for a button. Thereafter, Pritchard advertised
that his wares were 'made at night by fairies'.
The real reason for the completed waistcoat
was far more mundane. Pritchard's assistants
had been out Saturday night drinking heavily

Nos 43-45 Westgate Street. Note the false windows
on the Georgian façade.

and had used the shop to sleep off their stupor.
On Sunday morning, they were reluctant to
emerge in front of churchgoers and so finished
the waistcoat off to pass the time.

Five

TUDOR AND STUART GLOUCESTER: UPHEAVAL AND CHANGE

THE TUDOR AND Stuart period in Gloucester could be described as one of upheaval and great change. The religious turmoil was particularly evident during the reign of Mary I and the martyrdom of Gloucester's second bishop, John Hooper. During the English Civil War, Gloucester was a Parliamentarian stronghold and withstood Charles I's assault upon the city. Indeed, the king's failure to take Gloucester proved a turning point in the history of the Civil War. Also during this period, the now-familiar coat of arms were drawn up. This period leaves behind a number of interesting buildings and monuments that can still be seen today.

Bishop Hooper and Hooper's Monument

The monument to Bishop Hooper, located between St Mary de Lode church and the western gateway to the cathedral precincts, marks the location of his martyrdom, which took place on 9 February 1555. Hooper, who had been Bishop of Gloucester and was a staunch Protestant, was burnt at the stake during the reign of 'Bloody Mary'.

The statue was unveiled in 1863 and is the work of Edward W. Thornhill (of Dublin). The 8ft-high statue, constructed of Portland Stone, is housed in a canopy in the Decorated style by architects Medland and Maberley;

composition of the canopy was undertaken by Oliver Eatcourt, a local builder. The monument replaced an earlier and more modest statue to Hooper by James Cleavland of Bangor, which dated from 1826. Some £400 was raised by public subscription to pay for the canopy. An additional 100 guineas was, again, raised by public subscription to fund the statue.

John Hooper was originally from Somerset and educated at Oxford, gaining a BA in 1519. Sometime afterwards, he entered the Cistercian monastery at

Cleve, Somerset, where he remained until Sir Thomas Arundel's visitation in 1537. Arundel was one of Thomas Cromwell's commissioners for the suppression of religious houses and it was Arundel who introduced Hooper to the work of Continental reformers Huldrick Zwingli and Henrich Bullinger. It was to prove the turning point in his life. Henry VIII's limited reforms to the English church and Hooper's increasingly Protestant views caused the latter to flee the realm in 1544, eventually settling in the Protestant refugee community in Zurich. It was not until the ascension of Edward VI to the throne, when the changes to the Church gathered momentum, that Hooper felt able to return to England to champion Protestant reforms.

Within a year of Hooper's return to England, he was appointed chaplain to John Dudley, Earl of Warwick and president of the council to Edward VI. This gave Hooper access to the royal court, where he was looked on favourably and respectfully by the young king, and where he became a regular preacher.

In March 1550, Hooper preached a Lenten sermon in which he appeared to attack the Church's ordinal concerning the ordination of priests and deacons. Firstly, Hooper asserted that candidates were required to swear by the saints, which he saw as idolatrous. Secondly, he challenged the wearing of white vestments, since he could not find any passage in scripture (or in the practice of the Primitive Church) that called for its use. His final objection concerned the use of a particular ceremonial, namely, 'where and of whom and when have they learned that he that is called to the ministry of God's word, should hold the bread and chalice in one hand and the book in the other hand?'

Again, Hooper could find no scriptural evidence for the practice or any that it was used in the early church. Although these details, through modern eyes, may seem trivial, it reveals Hooper's belief in the sufficiency of Scripture and the ideal of the New Testament Church. Furthermore, it is evidence that Hooper wanted to rid the English Church of all vestiges of Roman Catholicism that he regarded as a departure from the word of God. Shortly after Hooper preached the third sermon, he was summoned before Thomas Cranmer, Archbishop of Canterbury; nevertheless he lost no favour at court.

At Easter of that year, the king and council informed Hooper that he was to be granted the bishopric of Gloucester. Hooper, however, initially refused. This action was highly unusual and, by rejecting the offer, Hooper was effectively saying 'no' to the king. Furthermore, this was technically illegal under the Act of Uniformity, passed a year earlier. It was a real possibility that Hooper could have been fined a year's income and imprisoned. Hooper explained, in a letter to Heinrich Bullinger, that he had taken the decision because of 'the shameful and impious form of the oath, which all who choose to undertake the function of a bishop are compelled to put up with, and also on account of those Aaronic habits which they still retain in that calling, and are used to wear, not only at the administration of the sacraments, but also at public prayers'. In short, Hooper rejected the bishopric of Gloucester as he found the vestments that he had to wear unscriptural.

Unsurprisingly, it did not take long before Hooper was summoned before the king to explain himself. The king accepted Hooper's arguments but, despite the Edward's lenience, an increasingly heated debate raged between Hooper, the bishops and the council that advised the young king. Cranmer referred the matter to Nicholas Ridley, Bishop of London. Ridley, who saw Hooper as a somewhat destructive force in the Church, succeeded in turning a number of council members against him, with the result that Hooper grew more obstinate over the issue than ever. Matters came to a head by the end of the year and Hooper was ordered to spend two weeks at Lambeth Palace in the company of Cranmer. When this failed to have effect, Hooper was committed to Fleet Prison. The Fleet was known as a debtor's prison and was notorious both for the poor conditions inside and for the stench from the open sewer that ran beside it. On 15 February 1551, Hooper sent a letter to the archbishop, which – although it did not mention vestments by name, referring instead to 'external things' – was contrite enough to secure his release. On 8 March, Hooper was consecrated Bishop of Gloucester at Lambeth Palace by Cramner, assisted by Ridley and John Ponet, the Bishop of Rochester. All bishops were attired in the white vestments as prescribed by the ordinal. Given Hooper's aversion to this garment, it is somewhat ironic that Thornhill's statue of Hooper depicts him in the self-same vestments that he had fought so hard not to wear.

Two weeks later, Hooper was installed at Gloucester. The tone of his episcopy was set in a pastoral letter addressed to all clergy in the diocese. It was clear that Hooper was going to be a hands-on bishop who was zealous in reform. The pastoral letter reminded clergy of their high calling and of the scriptural qualities that he expected them to possess.

Furthermore, along with his letter, Hooper sent fifty articles of faith, which he expected every priest to observe. During his first visit of the diocese, Hooper drew up thirty-one injunctions to regulate church life. One of these was to ensure that the prayer book was read audibly and that the congregation could hear their minister. This was a swipe at the priestly muttering in Latin of the Catholic Church Mass, which deeply offended many Protestants. Additionally, when the church windows came to be repaired, no image of any saint was permitted and transubstantiation was not to be defended, publicly or privately. Hooper's reforms were clearly aimed at removing any vestiges of Catholicism.

It is not clear how effective Hooper was in bringing about his ideals during his tenure as bishop. For example, during his first visitation, William Phelps of Cirencester was found to hold Catholic views of the Eucharist. Phelps made a public submission after meeting with Hooper yet, following the accession of Mary I to the throne a few years later, Phelps recanted and moved back to his earlier position. No doubt, Phelps was motivated by his desire to hold on to the living.

Some 311 ministers were examined in Hooper's visitation. Sixty-eight were unable to recite the Ten Commandments and thirty-one could not say where in the Bible they could be found. Forty clerics were not able to recite the Lord's Prayer. The figures show the poor standards of education amongst many of the diocese's clergy at the time. That said, it was probably no better or worse than the situation in other dioceses.

Another feature of Hooper's tenure of the bishopric was that the Consistory Court sat for more times than under any

Bishop Hooper's monument,
St Mary's Square.

other Bishop of Gloucester before or since. The Consistory Court dealt with spiritual matters, and meted out various forms of public penance for those found guilty. On some occasions, the penitents were required to be placed in a 'whyche', that is, a cell at the High Cross, in the centre of Gloucester. A notice of their offence was placed on their forehead and the penitent would be required to announce their transgression to anyone who passed by.

On 24 October 1551, Nicholas Heath, the traditionalist Bishop of Worcester, was deprived of his office. This left the question of who to replace him and it was decided that Hooper was also be given the bishopric of Worcester, with the two dioceses becoming merged.

The accession of Mary I to the throne marked a turning point in Hooper's life that would ultimately lead to his martyrdom. Hooper, despite his hatred of Catholicism, did not support the attempt by the Duke of Northumberland (John Dudley) to install Lady Jane Grey as queen. Rather, Hooper's belief in the doctrine of Christian obedience led him to call upon the people of Gloucestershire and Worcestershire to support Mary. With Mary now sovereign, it was not long before the tide turned in favour of Catholicism. On 2 August 1553, Hooper received a summons for his 'undelayed repair' to the court of Mary I. On 26 August, he sat for the last time at the Consistory Court, before starting out on the journey to London. Hooper was summoned to appear before Mary at Richmond on 29 August, on charges that he owed the queen money. Three days later, on 1 September, Hooper was committed, once again, to the Fleet. He was never to gain his liberty again.

It was now only a matter of time before Hooper would learn of his eventual fate. During his imprisonment, Hooper was occasionally able to smuggle letters and tracts to his supporters. One such was to Joan Wilkinson, of King's Stanley, Gloucestershire, exhorting her 'to rejoice in such troubles as shall happen unto you for the truth's sake: for in that part Christ saith you be happy'. Encouraging his Protestant supporters using words from Scripture was a common feature of Hooper's letters from prison, as the letter to Joan Wilkinson shows.

In March 1554, Hooper was deprived of his bishopric and concerted efforts were made to discredit him by claiming that he had recanted, but these efforts largely failed.

On 22 January 1555, Hooper was arraigned at St Saviour's church, Southwark, and Hooper was again examined at length by a commission headed by Stephen Gardiner, the Bishop of Winchester. They found Hooper obstinate, that is, Hooper refused to recant his Protestantism. The next day, Gardiner pronounced the sentence of execution and Hooper was transferred to Newgate Prison. On 4 February, Edmund Bonner, Bishop of London, carried out the process of degrading (or defrocking) Hooper. Apparently, Hooper expressed great joy when he was told that Gloucester was to be the place of his execution. He was handed over to six guards who were charged with escorting him back to the city.

Hooper arrived in Gloucester during the early evening of Thursday, 7 February and crowds began to gather on the approach to the city to see him pass by. The guards sought additional assistance from the mayor, fearing that an attempt might be made to free their prisoner, and the mayor sent troops to the North Gate and ordered people to stay indoors.

Hooper spent the night at the home of Robert and Agnes Ingram, located opposite St Nicholas' church in Westgate Street (and now Gloucester Folk Museum). The following day (8 February), he received a number of visitors. The first was Sir Anthony Kingston, who became a convinced Protestant after costly dealings with Hooper in the Consistory Court. Kingston tried in vain to persuade Hooper to accept the queen's mercy, in order that he would save his own life by recanting. Hooper replied that:

> True it is matter Kingston, that death is bitter, and life is sweet: but, alas, consider that the death to come is more bitter, and the life to come is more sweet. Therefore, for the desire and love I have of the one, and the terror and fear of the other, I do not so much regard this death, nor esteem this life, but have settled myself, through the strength of God's Holy Spirit, patiently to pass through the torments and extremities of the fire now prepared for me rather than to deny the truth of his word, desiring you and others, in the meantime, to commend me to God's mercy in your prayers.

His second visitor was Thomas Drowry, a blind boy, who had recently been imprisoned for maintaining Protestant beliefs. On hearing that Hooper was back in Gloucester, Drowry had pleaded with his jailers to be allowed to visit him, and was granted his request. Hooper said of Drowry: 'God hath taken from thee thy outward sight, for what reason he best knowesth but he hath given thee another sight much more precious, for he hath endued thy soul with the eyes of knowledge and faith.' The following year, on 15 May 1556, Drowry, along with Thomas Croker, a bricklayer, was also burnt at the stake.

That evening, Hooper was visited by Thomas Bell, the mayor, as well as William Jenkins and William Bond, town sheriffs and the aldermen of the council. Friendliness was exhibited amongst the group and Hooper asked the sheriffs for a quick fire in order to lessen his suffering. After this meeting, Hooper retired to bed at 5 p.m. in order to spend the night in prayer.

The place of his execution, between St Mary de Lode's church and the thirteenth-century St Mary's Gate, seems to have been chosen with some thought. The site was overlooked by the cathedral and the windows above the gate where he taught his students to guard against 'pestilent heresies'. The location, therefore, perhaps added a touch of irony to his execution.

On the morning of 9 February, Hooper borrowed a gown and hat from Robert Ingram to be walked to his place of execution, only a short distance away. As it was a Saturday, the market was bustling and many people came to see the burning of their former pastor. Hooper was allowed to pray quietly for half an hour before he was fastened to the stake. One iron ring was used for this purpose. However, it barely fitted – the poor prison conditions had caused Hooper's stomach to swell and he had to hold himself in so that the iron band could be fastened around his waist. As was the custom, the executioner came forward to ask forgiveness from the condemned man and Hooper gave it.

Detail of Bishop Hooper's monument.

Bishop Hooper's Lodging (No. 100 Westgate Street). It is thought this was where Hooper spent his last night. It is now the Folk Museum.

Sadly, Hooper was not to be granted his wish for a quick fire. The wood used was green and took some time to light. Moreover, as the flames rose around Hooper, a strong wind blew the fire out, leaving Hooper only mildly burned. A second attempt was similarly unsuccessful, burning Hooper's lower body and singeing his hair. During Mary's reign, individuals condemned to be burnt were allowed to have bladders of gunpowder fastened under each arm. This was deemed an act of mercy; intended to decrease the time of suffering and hasten death. The third attempt to start the fire around Hooper finally reached these bladders. However, the explosives broke open and failed to ignite, almost certainly because they were damp. Finally, after three-quarters of an hour, Hooper made his last prayer, calling out, 'Lord Jesus have mercy upon me! Lord Jesus have mercy upon me! Lord Jesus, receive my Spirit!' and, shortly, afterwards, he died. Hooper's Lodging, now the Folk Museum (No. 100 Westgate Street), contains the charred stake on which he was burnt.

'The Old Judges House', No. 26 Westgate Street

One of Gloucester's hidden gems is No. 26 Westgate Street, which is also known as 'The Old Judges House' on account of it being used as a lodging for assize court judges during the early nineteenth century. The façade was remodelled in about 1815 and conceals a magnificent sixteenth- and seventeenth-century town house. A walk down Maverdine Lane, a narrow passage to the east of the building, reveals a timber elevation, four storeys high, with five gables, overhangings and oriel windows.

Created in around 1815, the façade of No. 26 Westgate Street hides a magnificent sixteenth-century timber-framed merchant's house.

Maverdine Lane reveals the magnificent timber framing.

It is possible that the house may have been the headquarters for Colonel Edward Massey, who successfully resisted the Royalist Siege of Gloucester in 1643. However, it is also possible that Massey's headquarters were actually located on the site of the Old Crown, further down Westgate Street.

St Mary de Crypt Grammar School

Adjoining St Mary de Crypt church is the schoolroom, erected in 1539 by John and Joan Cook as a 'contynuall free scole of grammer'. The school remained there until 1861 when it transferred to buildings in Barton Street. In 1944 the school moved again, to a new site in Podsmead Lane. The original grammar school buildings were restored by C.G. Marylard and reopened in 1880 as a Sunday school. Above the archway and below the oriel window of the school are the arms of King Henry VIII. John and Joan Cooke's memorial can be found next door, in St Mary de Crypt church (*see* St Mary de Crypt Church p. 33).

The Old Bell, No. 9 Southgate Street

The most striking feature from the outside is the magnificent (restored) Jacobean timber-panelled façade. The property was built for Thomas Yate, an alderman and apothecary, in 1664. There is a suggestion that the timber may have come from the Pilgrim Fathers' ship the *Mayflower*. This ship was owned by the Berkeley family and salt deposits have been found behind some of the beams. During the eighteenth century it was known as the Old Blue Shop because the owner – James Lee, a tobacconist and blue maker – painted the house bright blue. Later, the house became part of the Bell Hotel, which stood next door. The Bell Hotel was first mentioned in 1544 and was demolished during 1969 to make way for the Eastgate Street Shopping Centre. This house was also the birthplace of George Whitefield, who became a famous Calvinist Methodist leader.

The magnificent front consists of three levels, jettied at the first and the second floors. The first-floor windows have triangular pediments containing shell motifs. At the second-floor level, a number of grotesques can be seen. Inside the building, on the first floor, a splendid fireplace surround is located. It dates from 1650, which is earlier than the rest of the house, and possibly commemorates Yate's first marriage. At the base of the overmantel there are four cherubs, which are supposed to be Yate's sons. A closer inspection will also reveal that the second boy from the left has six fingers on one hand, which is also said to be true of one of Yate's sons. The fireplace also has the coat of arms of Yate's family in the centre of the mantelpiece, along with the coats of arms of the Box and Berkeley families on the left and on the right, below.

Later owners of the building include Henry Yates Jones Taylor, who was born here in March 1826. He would go on to record the eccentric and unusual stories of times past from older residents of Gloucester. The stories were then published in the local newspapers. At the turn of the century, the building was in the possession of a Mr Clark, a tea merchant. Clark promoted his business with a large metal tea canister set above the parapet of the building.

St Mary de Crypt church and the original Crypt Grammar School established by John and Joan Cooke in 1539.

The arms of Henry VIII, on St Mary de Crypt Grammar School.

Upper storeys of The Old Bell (No. 9 Southgate Street).

Gloucester and the English Civil War

The English Civil War was a series of conflicts between King Charles I and Parliament. Those on the side of Parliament would become known as the Parliamentarians, although their enemies also referred to them as Roundheads – a name that derived from the closely cropped hair displayed by the predominantly pro-Parliamentarian Puritans. Those who supported Charles I became known as Royalists, or Cavaliers – a name deriving from the Latin *caballarius*, meaning horsemen. By the 1640s, relations had become so strained that the country descended into open warfare, with Charles I raising his standard at Nottingham on 22 August 1642. The first battle took place two months later, on 23 October 1642, at Edgehill in Warwickshire. Neither side were able to gain a decisive victory, however, and the civil war would rumble on for the next three years until the Royalists were finally defeated at the Battle of Naseby, on 24 June 1645. With the Royalist forces in disarray, Charles I fled north and surrendered to the Scots on 6 May. Unable to gain the support of the Scottish Presbyterians, Charles was eventually handed over to Parliament and faced execution on 30 January 1649.

Gloucester was a pro-Parliamentarian city in a mainly Royalist part of the country. Charles I had made his headquarters at Oxford and, by 1643, the Royalists had captured Tewkesbury, Marlborough, Malmsbury, Devizes, Salisbury and Chester. In July 1643, the Royalists seized Bath and Bristol following the Battle of Lansdown. Gloucester was then surrounded by Royalist-controlled land, yet Charles I's forces failed to capture this strategically important city.

The sundial on the chancel of St Mary de Crypt church, constructed to cover up damage sustained during the Siege of Gloucester.

Headless gargoyles on the west end of the nave in Gloucester Cathedral.

Gloucester was under the leadership of Lieutenant-Colonel Edward Massey, a professional soldier who refused to surrender despite being heavily outnumbered and the poor state of Gloucester's defences. On 10 August, some 30,000 Royalists were gathered around Gloucester. The Parliamentarian force numbered only 1,400, with a mere forty barrels of gunpowder and fortifications that saw earthworks reinforcing the gaps in the Roman walls. Although the Royalists had more than enough troops to storm the city, they were reluctant to do so, perhaps as a result of the heavy losses sustained during their attack on Bristol. Instead, they waited for Gloucester's citizens to be starved into submission. Massey, by contrast, was aggressive in defence and regularly sent out raiding parties to disrupt the Royalists, attacking their siege machines and stealing tools. This failed attempt by Royalists

to storm Gloucester is thought to have been preserved in a children's nursery rhyme: 'Humpy Dumpty'. The rhyme is believed to concern scaffolding erected to breach the city walls, which subsequently collapsed. The city walls were later pulled down on the orders of Charles II following the Restoration.

A number of stories have emerged regarding the Siege of Gloucester. One popular tale is of a pig that was poked and prodded to make it squeal in an effort to convince the Royalists that Gloucester still had plenty of food in the city.

After twenty-seven days under siege, a Parliamentarian army, led by the Earl of Essex, reached Prestbury Hill, only 10 miles from Gloucester. The Royalist forces, unwilling to be trapped between this army and the troops stationed at Gloucester garrison, decided to withdraw. They were unaware that Massey had only three barrels of gunpowder left.

A replacement gargoyle, created in 2013 by Pascal Mychalysin, the cathedral's mason.

What is remarkable is the lack of damage that Gloucester sustained during the siege. In part, the ineffectiveness of Royalist artillery may be put down to the fact that many shots were poorly aimed, while the reactions of Gloucester's residents were swift and quick-witted. Once, a grenade fell near the south gate, close to where a woman was carrying a pail of water. Thinking quickly, she doused the grenade with water, extinguishing its fuse.

Nonetheless, Gloucester still bears the scars of its Civil War encounters. One building to fall casualty to the ravages of the war was St Oswald's Priory, which was largely destroyed by Royalist canon fire. The ruins are still visible (*see* St Oswald's

Priory p. 40). Greyfriars Priory also suffered under artillery fire and much of the building was destroyed. Damage was likewise caused to St Nicholas' church spire (Westgate Street), (*see* St Nicholas' Church p. 36), while at St Mary de Crypt church (Southgate Street) the sundial on the chancel is said to have been commissioned to hide the marks of war (*see* St Mary de Crypt Church p. 33). Gloucester Cathedral displays some of the damage wrought by the Parliamentarians themselves, who attacked perceived popery within the city: many of the gargoyles are headless where they were used for target practice and the stonework on the south aisle shows impact marks from musket balls.

Scriven's Conduit

Scriven's Conduit.

Scriven's Conduit, located in Hillfield Garden's, London Road, was originally located in Southgate Street, close to the junction of Longsmith Street. The elaborately carved edifice was erected in 1636 by Alderman John Scriven to supply the area with fresh water from Robinswood Hill. Before the construction of the conduit, residents used a tap at The Cross or took water directly from their own wells. The well water in the area at this time was apparently known for its 'sparkling properties' because of the leaching of ammonia from cesspits.

The conduit was taken down in 1784 and rebuilt in a garden in Clarence Street. In around 1839 it was moved once more, and re-erected in the grounds of Edgeworth Manor, near Cirencester. In 1937, the conduit was returned to Gloucester and established in its present location.

The octagonal conduit is constructed of Painswick Stone and is designed with a mixture of Gothic and Classical forms. A Gothic arcade supports a slender parapet from which ogee ribs rise to support a finial. This is much weathered and it said to be a depiction of Jupiter Pluvius pouring rainwater on to Sabrina. It is thought that the top of the structure may have been rebuilt in 1705. Above each of the arches, friezes depict a number of industries that could be found in the Severn Vale. These industries include: cider making, fishing and corn and wool production.

Charles II Statue

St Mary's Square was almost entirely rebuilt in 1959–61 by J.V. Wall, the city architect. The first, southernmost section of flats focuses on a weathered statue of Charles II. It is thought that the sculptor was Stephen Baldwin and the statue dates from 1662. Originally positioned in a niche at the former Wheat Market, in Southgate Street, it was removed when the Wheat Market was demolished in the eighteenth century. The statue was believed to be lost until 1945 when it was rediscovered in a garden at Chaxhill, Westbury-on-Severn. It was erected in its present position in the 1960s.

Twenty-two listed houses were demolished to make way for the new flats in St Mary's Square. These included a group of fifteenth-century timber-framed cottages. A number of carved-figure bracelets are preserved at the nearby Gloucester Folk Museum on Westgate Street.

Queen Anne Statue

The Queen Anne statue, sculpted by John Ricketts the Elder in 1711–12, is located in the Spa Ground. Now severely weathered, it once stood at the northern end of the Wheat Market in Southgate Street. In around 1780, the statue was moved from Southgate Street to the garden of Paddock House, Pitt Street and in 1839 it was taken from there to College Green. In 1865, the statue was removed to its present location.

Greyfriars House

Greyfriars House was built in 1610 for Philo Maddy, a Gloucester currier (a dealer in leather). The building consists of an ashlar façade with a central pediment and a portico with Doric columns. It replaced an earlier building of the same name that belonged to Sir John Powell, a judge and politician. Powell, born in 1645, was educated at Oxford, entered the Inner Temple in 1664 and was called to the bar in 1671. He was active in local politics and became a common councilman of Gloucester from 1672, also serving as town clerk between 1674–85 and 1687–91. In 1685, he was elected to Parliament by the freemen

CHARLES II
This statue was carved in 1662 by Stephen Baldwyn
and was set up in the Wheat Market in Southgate Street
It was removed in the middle of the eighteenth century
and its whereabouts remained obscure until 1945 when
it was re-discovered in pieces in a garden at Chax Hill.
Re-erected in this position, 1960

Charles II statue, St Mary's Square.

Greyfriars House.

of Gloucester. His legal career continued to advance and he was crested a serjeant-at-law in 1689 and a baron of the exchequer on 31 October 1691. On 4 October 1691, Powell received a knighthood and, upon the accession of Queen Anne to the throne, he was promoted to the Queen's Bench.

One of Powell's most notable cases was the prosecution of Jane Wenham in 1712 on the charge of witchcraft. However, when the verdict of guilt was given against her, Powell delivered the death sentence but also expressed doubts about the evidence supplied. This helped to ensure that Wenham's sentence was later reprieved, and Powell would go on to secure a royal pardon for her. During the trial it had been alleged that

Wenham was able to fly, to which Powell reputedly commented that 'There is no law against flying'. Jane Wenham would be the last person to be convicted of witchcraft in the country.

Powell died in Gloucester on 14 June 1713. Most of his estate was settled on the marriage of John Snell with his niece Anna Maria, which took place earlier in 1713. Powell was buried in the Lady chapel of Gloucester Cathedral. His grave is marked by an excellent standing monument by Thomas Green of Camberwell. Powell is depicted standing, dressed in the robes of the Queen's Bench. The effigy of Powell is carved in white marble set against a black background, in a shell-headed recess flanked by Corinthian pilasters.

The Cherubs from Booth Hall, and the Coat of Arms

The more usual form of Gloucester's coat of arms.

Gloucester's coat of arms can be found all around the city: they appear on many of the city's municipal buildings, on the blue plaques that signify antiquarian interests and at Gloucester Rugby Club. An eighteenth-century version of the arms, together with two cherubs, has been attached to the modern block (c. 1961) facing Three Cocks Lane where it meets Westgate Street. It was carved by Thomas Ricketts and once adorned the pediment of Booth Hall, which stood opposite to where Shire Hall now stands. Booth Hall was demolished in 1957.

In 1652, Sir Edward Bysshe assigned the coat of arms to the city during the herald's visitation of Gloucestershire. The gold shield comprises three red chevrons with ten

The cherubs from Booth Hall.

torteau (roundels). The crest comprises a red demi-lion with a broadsword in the right paw and a trowel in the left paw, and red lion supporters (on either side of the shield) that hold broadswords in their right forepaws. The Latin inscription 'Fides Invicta Trimphant' can be translated as 'Unconquered Faith Triumphs'.

Since coats of arms were issued during the Commonwealth, they were declared null and void following the Restoration of Charles II to the throne. However, since the right to use the shield was granted during the reign of Charles I, the Corporation continued to use the arms and this situation went unchallenged in the following centuries. The Corporation chose to regularise the legality of their coat of arms and, consequently, they were recorded by the College of Arms and legally granted by letters patent on 16 April 1945.

St Nicholas' House

St Nicholas' House is next door to the church from which it gets its name. The eighteenth-century façade hides an earlier fifteenth-century townhouse. Once owned by the Whittingtons, the most famous member of this family – immortalised in a well-known fairy tale – is Richard or Dick Whittington. Richard was the son of Sir William Whittington of Gloucester, he was born in the village of Pauntley and, later, he was apprenticed to a London mercer. His fortune grew and he served as Lord Mayor of London on a number of occasions. Although the reasons remain obscure, the legend of Dick Whittington and his cat grew up in the seventeenth century, following the publication of the story in 1605.

Here Whittington is depicted as an orphan, who, believing that the streets of London are paved with gold, heads to the city to seek his fortune. Whittington, however, ends up cold and hungry, and falls asleep on at the door of Mr Fitzwarren, a rich merchant. Fitzwarren takes Whittington in and employs him as a scullery boy. Later Whittington travels aboard his master's ship and lands in a kingdom overrun with rats, at which point he sells his cat for ten times the value of the ship's cargo and makes his fortune. Sadly, it is not known whether the real Dick Whittington ever owned a cat. The Dick Whittington story is also told at the local Folk Museum, which contains a stone carving of a boy holding a cat, found at St Nicholas' House.

Six

THE EIGHTEENTH
CENTURY

George Whitefield

GEORGE WHITEFIELD, a Calvinist Methodist leader, was born in Gloucester on 15 December 1714 and was baptised at St Mary de Crypt church. His father was the proprietor of the Bell Inn, which once stood in Southgate Street. In 1967, the Bell Hotel, as it was known by then, was demolished to make way for the Eastgate Shopping Centre.

Whitefield was two years old when his father died. His mother remarried Capel Langdon but the marriage was not a happy one. Whitefield, aged 11, attended the Gloucester Cathedral School and a year later he was attending St Mary de Crypt Grammar School. However, the following year, Whitefield had to leave to assist with menial tasks at the Bell Inn because of his stepfather's financial mismanagement of the business. Whitefield was only able to return to St Mary de Crypt Grammar School after his mother separated from Langdon during the 1720s. Whitefield then attended Oxford University, gaining a BA in 1736. Whilst at Oxford, he attended the Oxford Holy Club. Members, which included Charles Wesley, the founder of the Methodist movement, were expected to devote themselves to prayer and other personal austerities.

Whitefield was ordained deacon by Bishop Benson of Gloucester on 20 June 1736. He preached his first sermon the Sunday afterwards and the pulpit from which he preached still stands in St Mary de Crypt church (see St Mary de Crypt Church p. 33).

Whitefield was well known as a preacher and began to undertake a number of missionary activities, both in Great Britain and in America. For the remainder of his life, Whitefield would divide his time between Britain and the American colonies. In 1738, Whitefield preached his first open-air sermon at Stonehouse, near Stroud, a few miles south of Gloucester. From 1739, Whitefield began to find Church of England pulpits barred to him because of his association with Nonconformists. Whitefield also regularly published his sermons in order to fund his missionary work. A constant theme was the necessity of 'new birth' in Christ Jesus and Whitefield proclaimed that those who did not accept this requisite would be condemned to hell. His sermons were perfected by repetition and he was able to use his voice and gestures to great effect. Whitefield would also show tears during his sermons. As Charles Wesley put it: his 'head

as waters' and his 'eyes as a fountain of tears'. If Whitefield would use tears to express the message he was extolling during his sermons, he would also expect them of his hearers. For Whitefield, this was a litmus test for how his sermons were received.

In 1741, he married Elizabeth James, a widow from Abergavenny. Whilst the couple were staying at the Bell Inn, Gloucester, in 1744 (which was now in the ownership of Whitefield's elder brother, Richard), their 4-month-old son died. The child was buried in St Mary de Crypt. Whitefield died on 30 September 1777 at Newburyport, Massachusetts. It is thought that, in his lifetime, Whitefield preached on 18,000 occasions.

Robert Raikes

Robert Raikes (1735–1811), promoter of the Sunday school movement and proprietor of the *Gloucester Journal*, was born within the shadow of the cathedral, at No. 7 Miller's Green. This address would later become the residence of all Gloucester Cathedral organists, including S.S. Wesley (*see* No. 7 Millers Green pp. 23–24). In 1767, Raikes married Anne Trigge and together they had three sons and seven daughters. Two of these children died in infancy: a son and a daughter.

In 1757, Raikes had succeeded his father as the owner of *Gloucester Journal* and continued to use the newspaper to highlight the poor conditions at Gloucester Prison. In 1768, *Gloucester Journal* carried an appeal on behalf of prisoners, particularly those convicted of lesser offenses. At this time, no allowance was made to support lesser offenders, who had to survive by sharing the rations

of their fellows. Raikes made many visits to the prison: assisting prisoners with the necessities of life, giving moral and religious instruction and helping some of them to find jobs. In 1773, he offered hospitality to John Howard, a prison reform campaigner who was touring prisons in the west of England to publicise the abuses that he found. In 1784, Gloucester Prison, which had been located in the old medieval castle, was given over to the Crown and a new gaol was erected on the site to be run on new and improved lines.

A number of stories try to explain the origin of Sunday schools in the city. The mostly commonly told suggests that Raikes was attempting to procure the services of a gardener and happened to be in the vicinity of St Catherine's Fields, on the outskirts of the city. This was one of the city's poorer areas and Raikes became concerned when he saw raggedly dressed local children playing coarse games in the street. The gardener's wife informed Raikes that it was worse on Sundays, when the street was full of children who were running wild and swearing and, apparently, indulging in gambling games. During the rest of the week, the children were employed at a pin factory. Raikes blamed the children's behaviour on ignorance stemming from their deprived background. From this encounter with the children of St Catherine's Street, the idea of a Sunday school began to form.

Somewhat less charitably, it has also been suggested – perhaps by Raikes' detractors – that he was disturbed by noisy children whilst reading his proofs. It is also possible that Raikes could have drawn on a number of precedents. For example, the Revd Joseph Alleine (1634–68), known as 'the Puritan father', drew young pupils together for religious instruction on Sunday. Raikes may, similarly, have heard of Mrs Catherine Bovey of Flaxley, Gloucestershire, who until her death, in 1726, would care for half a dozen poor children each Sunday, providing them with a good dinner and encouraging them to learn to recite the Catechism.

It has also been suggested that Raikes may have got the idea from William King, a Protestant Dissenter from Dursley, Gloucestershire, and a follower of George Whitefield. King is said to have contacted Raikes and, following an invitation to dinner, proposed his Sunday school scheme. Later, the two men went for a walk in the city and visited one of the poorer districts. Here they witnessed the squalid conditions of the people living there, with many wearing rags and unable to dress themselves decently. The local inhabitants lounged in the public road: fighting, screaming and swearing at each other, or engaging in entertainments including cock fighting and boxing. Raikes is said to have exclaimed, 'What a pity it is – what a shame to our country – that the Sabbath should be so desecrated!' King replied that the only option was for Raikes to open a Sunday school, similar to the one that King had already opened in Dursley. Raikes was apparently concerned that the Established Church might refuse to take up an idea that had originated from a Dissenter. Whatever the truth concerning the origins of the Sunday schools, it is certainly true that Raikes was not the originator of the idea. It is also true that he met with Thomas Stock shortly afterwards and that the two men worked together to establish a series of Sunday schools in Gloucester.

Thomas Stock (1749–1803) was headmaster of the grammar school in St Catherine's parish. He was also a curate of St John the Baptist church, Gloucester. Stock had previously established a Sunday school at Ashbury in Berkshire and, following a conversation with Raikes, it was agreed that they would establish at least four Sunday schools in the area. Stock drew up a list of rules and four women of good repute were employed as schoolmistresses. The first school to open was in St Catherine's Street, in the parish of the same name, and a Mrs King was given charge. The second school stood at the corner of Greyfriars and Southgate Street, in Raikes' own parish of St Mary de Crypt. The third opened in the back of No. 103 Northgate Street, and then a fourth was established in Oxbody Lane. The women were paid 1s 6d for their services, with Raikes supplying the shilling and Stock the 6d. Stock travelled to each school in

Robert Raikes.

the afternoon to catechise and examine the children, while Raikes tended to confine his attention to the school in his own parish of St Mary de Crypt. Initially, the schools only allowed boys to be admitted but soon afterwards girls were also admitted.

Raikes' personal invitations to parents to send their children to the new Sunday schools played a part in their success. On the opening of the first school, Raikes also took the time to go around his parish urging the parents to send their children to the school. Many parents replied that they were too poor to fit their children out in suitable clothing but Raikes asserted that if the clothing was good enough for the street, then it was fit enough for his school. Raikes went go on to say that he did not mind what rags they came in, so long as they attended with 'clean faces, clean hands, and their hair combed'. Raikes was certainly successful and, according to tradition, he became known as 'Bobby Wild Goose', after he was seen at the head of his young pupils as they were led from the school into church.

Raikes waited three years before publicising his Sunday school scheme at a time when there was a noticeable improvement in the children's behaviour on the streets of Gloucester. Raikes anonymously published the following in the *Gloucester Journal*: 'Some of the clergy in different parts, bent on attempting reform, are establishing Sunday schools for the rendering of the Lord's Day subservient to the ends of instruction which has hitherto been prostituted to bad purposes.' The article went on to comment on the changes of behaviour seen in the children. A number of enquiries stemmed from the article and Raikes' reply to a Colonel Richard Townley of

Rochdale, Yorkshire, was published in the *Gentleman's Magazine* in June 1784. Raikes explained that:

> I am generally at church, and after service they all come to make their bow, and, if any animosities have arisen, to make their complaint. The great principle I incalculate is to be kind and good-natured to each other; not to provoke one another; to be dutiful to their parents; not to offend God by cursing and swearing; and such little precepts as may all comprehend.

On 5 June 1784, Raikes wrote a letter to a Bradford-based enquirer, stating that:

> I have not had leisure to give the public an earlier account of my plan for reform of the rising generation by establishing Sunday schools where poor children may be received the Sunday and there engaged their learning to read and repeat the Catechism or anything else that may be deemed proper to open their minds to a knowledge of their duty to God, their neighbours, and themselves.

Letters such as these help to explain the rise of Sunday schools, with others able to imitate the concept. The rapid spread of Sunday schools across the country was also noted by John Wesley. While preaching in Binley he recorded in his journal that, 'I find these schools springing up everywhere I go' (18 June 1784).

Raikes believed that Anglicans ought to take a lead on the issue. His friend Dr Samuel Glasse, preaching a sermon at St Mary's church, Painswick, claimed that 200,000 children were now being taught in Sunday schools and encouraged the trend to continue. Painswick church was packed and the congregation – who chiefly consisted of artisans and farmers, and who managed to completely fill the church – were most generous in giving money to support the Sunday schools. At the service a collection was taken and £57 was raised – more than double the amount that Raikes had expected. The sermon was also published as *The Piety, Wisdom, and Policy of Promoting Sunday Schools* (1786), which helped to provide impetus to the Sunday school movem[ent].

William Fox, a Baptist, had been to establish a system of day school he heard of Raikes' Sunday school consulting Raikes, he decided th establishment of Sunday schools wo more practicable and he formed the S School Society in 1786, to help to est and support Sunday schools througho UK. Raikes supported and encourage although he did not attend any meeti the society. In 1787, Raikes was admitt the society as an honorary member, owi his zeal and the status Raikes held as founder of the Sunday school movement.

At Christmas 1786, Raikes was granted an audience with George III and Queen Charlotte to explain the Sunday school movement. Following the meeting, Queen Charlotte put measures in place to establish a number of Sunday schools throughout the country. Such royal patronage can only have increased support for this movement. During a visit by George III to Cheltenham in 1788, Madame D'Arblay (Frances Burney), a Keeper of Robes to the Queen, sought out Robert Raikes. In her diary, published after her death,

Robert Raikes's house in Southgate Street.
It is now a public house.

she recorded that she found Raikes 'somewhat too flourishing, somewhat too forward, somewhat too valuable, but he is witty, benevolent, good natured and goodhearted'.

Raikes died suddenly from a heart attack on 5 April 1811 and was buried in St Mary de Crypt church, in the family vault known as the 'Raikes Chapel'. He left instructions that the Sunday school should follow his remains to their resting place, and that each child to do so would receive a shilling and a plum cake.

There are a number of memorials associated with Robert Raikes in the city. In St Mary de Crypt church, a nineteenth-century boxwood plaque with a profile of Raikes is found in the north chapel. In the grounds of The Park, a statue to Robert Raikes was erected in 1930. It imitates the version erected on the London Embankment in 1880, which commemorated the hundredth anniversary since the first Sunday schools were established by Raikes and Stock. The London statue, sculpted by Sir Thomas Brock, was unveiled by the Earl of Shaftsbury on 3 July 1880. A large roundel with a three-quarter bust of Raikes can be found attached to the walls of the citizen offices in St John's Lane. It is by W.S. Frith and dates from 1884. The bust was originally on the façade of the Raikes Memorial Sunday Schools (since demolished), which adjoined the Baptist church in Brunswick Road.

The houses that Robert Raikes lived in are also still standing. Robert Raikes House (formerly known as the Golden Cross) on Southgate Street is now a public house. It was originally built as a merchant's house in the mid- to late sixteenth century and possesses an elaborate timber-framed frontage. Raikes lived there between 1768 and 1801 as well as living at the nearby Ladybellegate House, Ladybellegate Street.

Ladybellegate House

Ladybellegate House is a fine example of an eighteenth-century town house – perhaps the finest in Gloucester. It was built in 1704 by Henry Wagstaffe, on land that his grandfather had first leased. The house was sublet to the Raikes family between 1732 and 1772 (except during the period 1740–43). Hence it was once the residence of Robert Raikes the Elder, the founder of the *Gloucester Journal*, and Robert Raikes the Younger, the founder of the Sunday school movement (*see* Robert Raikes p. 79).

The house is well known for its ornamental plasterwork, resulting from the time that the house was let to Henry Guise of Elmore, who may also have been responsible for the remodelling to the front of the house when he leased the property between 1740 and 1743. Most of the rooms have moulded plaster panels with a swan crest – the family crest of the Guises. Jupiter is depicted on the staircase ceiling, seated in the clouds with an eagle. The hallway ceiling has heads, in roundrels, which represent the Greek philosophers.

During the nineteenth century, the Gloucester Liberal Club was founded here. In 1890, the Gloucester Friendly Society's Medical Association established a dispensary at the house, maintaining the services

Ladybellegate House.

of a doctor. Prior to the building of the new telephone exchange next door, Ladybellegate House was purchased by Post Office Telephones. The new telephone exchanged was opened in 1971 and Ladybellegate House was sold to the Gloucester Civic Trust for £1. The house was restored and reopened by HRH Princess Anne in 1979.

Bearland Lodge

Bearland Lodge, Longsmith Street was built in around 1720 for William Lane, a barrister. The pediment of the building contains a half-size figure of Perseus, in a billowing cloak and seated upon a lion. There is also a cherub and Perseus is holding a shield with the head of Medusa depicted on it. It is thought that this sculpture may have come from the nearby Ladybellegate House (*see* above). The sculpture is attributed to John Ricketts.

Bearland Lodge.

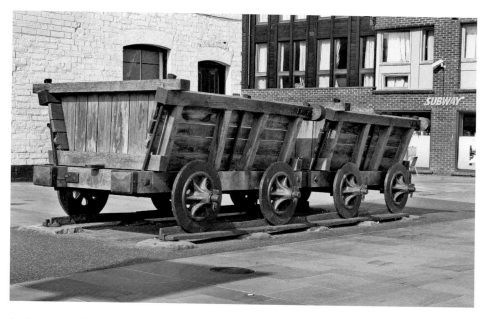

Replica wagons that were typically used on the tramway, along with a section of plate rail.

the tramway as goods, such as coal from the Forest of Dean bound for Cheltenham, could be transported along a connected railway network, avoiding transhipment at Gloucester.

A few remnants of the tramway can still be found in Gloucester. The entrance gateway of the tramway, leading to the docks from Southgate Street, is still in evidence and at the docks there are replica wagons of the type that were used on the line mounted on a short section of track. From Southgate Street, the tramway traversed Albion Street, before curving behind Brunswick Square in a section of tramway that is now know as Old Tram Road. The tracks then crossed the Birmingham to Gloucester railway at Horton Road. At the south side of the nearby Armscroft Park, an embankment, which carried the tramway, is still in evidence. Development from housing and road improvements have obliterated any other trace of the tramway in the city.

Gloucester Docks

Gloucester Docks are a remarkably complete example of a Victorian inland port. The warehouses, dating from 1827, are of an unusually uniform design; in part due to the conditions of the canal company leases and also because the buildings were erected primarily to store corn. The first seagoing vessels arrived in 1827 and Gloucester became a popular port, with many preferring to dock at Gloucester due to the lower import charges and the avoidance of transhipment at Bristol. In the 1860s a new and larger lock opened at Sharpness and allowed vessels to use the canal to travel to Gloucester. From the 1930s, petroleum was carried to Gloucester in order to serve the burgeoning number of motor vehicles. The movement of goods through Gloucester declined during the 1960s, with many cargoes switching to road transport. Coaster traffic also declined and goods traffic to the Port of Gloucester was effectively over by 1988. The last remaining regular goods traffic on the canal were grain barges passing through to Tewkesbury, a service that ran until 1998.

From the 1970s it was recognised that the traditional uses for the site were now in terminal decline and that new attractions were needed for the docks. Consequently, development has centred around the leisure industries and a number of warehouses were also converted into offices. A major setback occurred, in 1987, when the Britannia Warehouse caught fire and was severely damaged. The decision was taken to rebuild the warehouse, identical in appearance to the one that was lost. In 1988 the Waterways Museum, located in Llanthony Warehouse, was opened and development of the leisure facilities at the docks has continued, more recently with the opening of the Gloucester Quays Shopping Centre.

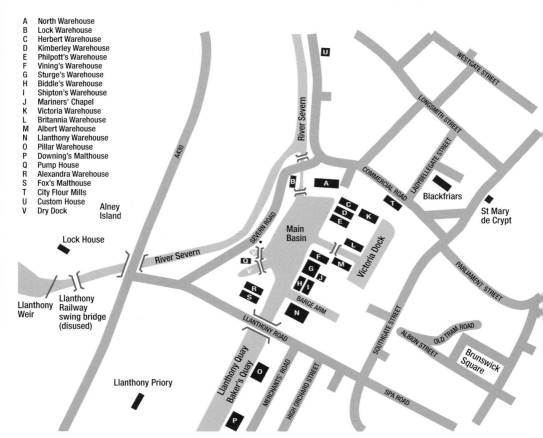

A North Warehouse
B Lock Warehouse
C Herbert Warehouse
D Kimberley Warehouse
E Philpott's Warehouse
F Vining's Warehouse
G Sturge's Warehouse
H Biddle's Warehouse
I Shipton's Warehouse
J Mariners' Chapel
K Victoria Warehouse
L Britannia Warehouse
M Albert Warehouse
N Llanthony Warehouse
O Pillar Warehouse
P Downing's Malthouse
Q Pump House
R Alexandra Warehouse
S Fox's Malthouse
T City Flour Mills
U Custom House
V Dry Dock

A map of the Gloucester Docks area.

The Gloucester and Sharpness Canal

The tidal River Severn, especially the section north of Sharpness, was regarded as treacherous and difficult to navigate owing to the strong currents caused by the ebb and flow of the tides. The tides also heavily restricted vessel movements to and from Gloucester, particularly when travelling downriver, as this section often required two high tides to navigate. In 1793, an Act of Parliament was obtained for the construction of a ship canal that bypassed this hazardous section of river. However, after five years, construction stopped. The canal was beset by numerous problems, including landowner disputes; dissatisfaction

A ship navigating the Gloucester and Sharpness Canal.

with Robert Mylne, the chief engineer; poor weather; and competition for labour. At this stage, only 5 miles of the canal had been built. Work to complete the canal did not resume until 1817, when construction of the remainder of the canal was overseen by Thomas Telford. By 1820, the canal had reached Saul, where it connected with the Stroudwater Canal. After further delays, the canal finally opened in 1827. The first two vessels to travel the length of the canal arrived at Gloucester on 26 April, where a huge crowd had gathered to watch their arrival.

When the Gloucester and Sharpness Canal was built, it was described as 16 miles long and 16ft deep. When tall sailing ships used the canal, the waterway was dredged to a depth of 18ft in order to accommodate the large keels of these ships. Later, the predominant traffic was steamers, which were flatter-bottomed and did not require the canal to be dredged to such a depth. When the canal was completed, it had sixteen bridges, plus one across Gloucester Lock. Today there are eighteen. The canal is also known for its classically styled bridgemen's houses which appear here.

The Main Basin

The main basin of the docks was constructed between 1794 and 1799, by gangs of men equipped with only spades and wheelbarrows. The wheelbarrows were pushed over planks of wood and the spoil tipped out to raise the surrounding land. This method of working enabled the basin to be excavated to a depth of 18ft. Canal historian Hugh Conway-Jones notes that the work must have been challenging, as five successive contractors were used during construction.

In 1812, a lock connecting the basin to the River Severn was constructed, allowing river vessels to use the basin. The move also enabled an easier transfer of goods on to the newly constructed Gloucester and Cheltenham Tramroad (*see* The Gloucester and Cheltenham Railway p. 90). The opening of the Gloucester and Sharpness Canal was occasioned by the ringing of church bells and the firing of guns, and a vast crowd assembled to witness the first two ships enter the basin. Gloucester's location, being so far inland, led to a sharp rise in the number of vessels using the basin.

The North Warehouse

In 1826–27, the North Warehouse was the first warehouse to be built on a site recommended by Thomas Telford, who was building the canal towards Sharpness. The building was designed by Bartin Haigh and a stone plaque on the front wall of the warehouse records that the builders were W. Rees and Sons. One of the considerations of the design was for different floors to be leased out to a range of merchants who imported wheat, barley and oats from Europe. The brick cellars were used to store imported wine. As time passed, it became more common for larger merchants to occupy an entire building.

On the corner of the North Warehouse is attached a former ship's bell, from the ship *Atlas*, which was rung by the watchman to signal the start and finish times of the dockers' working day. During the 1940s, the bell was transferred to a light tower at Shepperdine, on the Severn Estuary, in order to aid navigation during foggy weather. When the warehouse was restored during the 1980s, Gloucester Rotary Club and the Gloucester Civic Trust had the bell re-erected.

The North Warehouse.

The Steam Crane

At the north end of the main basin, in front of the North Warehouse, a steam crane stands on an isolated section of track. The crane was built in 1944 by Joseph Booth & Brothers, of Rodley, Leeds. It could lift up to 7.5 tons and is a typical, though late, example of the steam cranes in use around many of Britain's canal-side quays. It spent its working life at the South Shields Repair Yard, before coming to Gloucester in 1994.

Phillpotts, Kimberley and Herbert Warehouses

These warehouses were built during 1846, when a large increase of foreign corn was anticipated following the expected aboli-tion of the Corn Laws. The Corn Laws were a set of laws that protected cereal produc-ers in Britain from cheaper foreign imports by imposing high import dues on these goods. Phillpotts Warehouse was built for A.H. Phillpotts, a corn merchant. It was the first

The Steam Crane, in front of the North Warehouse.

of the three warehouses to be completed and, to mark its completion, seventy of the builders were entertained in a local tavern to celebrate the custom of 'house-rearing'. The building of Kimberley Warehouse was financed by Humphrey Brown and leased to J.P. Kimberley, another corn merchant. Herbert Warehouse takes its name from Samuel Herbert, a solicitor, who financed its construction.

Vinings, Reynolds, Biddle and Shipton Warehouses

The building of Vinings Warehouse, in 1840, was financed by the corn merchant C.J.Vinning, and designed by T.S. Hack of Bristol. Unlike the other warehouses, the building originally had a double-height ground floor, which was first used by iron merchants. Later, additional iron columns were inserted to carry an intermediate floor.

Reynolds Warehouse, constructed in 1840, is a double-warehouse, built for J. & C. Sturge, corn merchants. In 1927, the building was leased to J. Reynolds & Co., of Albert Flour Mills, from whom the building's name was taken.

Biddle Warehouse was built in 1830, designed by William Franklin of Stroud, for John Biddle, a Stroud miller. The windows in this building are larger than the other warehouses and have segmental heads. This design feature echoes many of the cloth mills in the Stroud area.

Shipton Warehouse, built in 1833, is almost identical and was financed by the merchant J.M. Shipton.

Fox's Malthouse, Alexandra, Llanthony and Great Western Warehouses

Fox's Malthouse and Alexandra Warehouse (designed by J.P. Moore) were built for J.E. and S.E. Fox, corn merchants, in 1870. When the warehouse was first built, it included a small engine house at the west end in order provide power for the elevators and to run a small mill. However, in 1875, a spark from the chimney of the engine house caused a fire to be started in the eaves of the warehouse, which was not brought under control until five hours later. Initially, the firemen who arrived on the scene were unable to put the fire out since their manually powered jets were not forceful enough to reach the upper floors of the warehouse. There was nothing that the firemen could do except watch until the fire reached the third floor and their water jets were in range of the fire. Consequently, in the new build, Alexandra Warehouse was built without overhanging eaves and the walls were extended to form parapets instead.

Llanthony Warehouse was the largest and last warehouse constructed for the docks. It was named after Llanthony Secunda Priory, located only a short distance away, and was designed by Capel N. Tripp for Wait James and Co., corn merchants. It cost £7,000 to build and a 'substantial meat tea' was given to the builders on completion. Llanthony Warehouse was threatened with demolition in 1971, when the quay wall moved forward and subsided into the basin. Fortunately, repairs were made without affecting the warehouse and in 1988 it was converted into the National Waterways Museum, which depicts the history of Britain's canals.

The Great Western Warehouse was financed by William Partridge, a corn merchant, in 1863. The name of the warehouse does not derive from the railway company of the same name but instead relates to the fact that it was very large and stood at the westernmost part of Gloucester Docks. The warehouse was used to store grain but, in its later years, sugar was also stored here. The quay to the south of Llanthony Warehouse was where a fire-float, *Salamander*, was moored

Llanthony Warehouse.

Alexandra Warehouse.

for many years and was used during the 1945 fire. *Salamander* was built by the firm Abdela & Mitchell of Brimscombe and contained six steam-powered hoses, capable of delivering up to 1,000 gallons of water per second. Underwater jets also provided a means of propulsion. When the fire broke out at the Great Western Warehouse, *Salamander* was positioned close to the warehouse. However, *Salamander*

was not tied up properly and, when the main hose was turned on, the fire-float swung round and the jet of water was unintentionally delivered to a crowd of bystanders, who had gathered on Llanthony Bridge. Eventually, the fire was brought under control, but not before extensive damage was done. Such was the damage that the building was converted into a single-storey warehouse.

Victoria Dock

The Corn Laws, which imposed heavy import dues on grain, were repealed in 1846 and enabled cheaper foreign imports of corn. The Victoria Dock was constructed to facilitate this expansion of imported grain. The site required a large excavation of spoil, which was then taken to Over Bridge for the expansion of the railway embankment. However, there were numerous complaints

A 10-ton manually operated crane at Victoria Dock.

about spoil dropping off the carts and fouling the roads, and magistrates warned drivers against overloading and 'furious driving'. Nonetheless, when the dock was formally opened on 18 April 1849, thousands of spectators watched as ten vessels entered the new dock bedecked with flags. The dock was also known as the Salt Basin and trains transported salt from Droitwich and Stoke Prior (both in northern Worcestershire) to the quay at the Victoria Dock. The salt was then transferred to ships bound for Continental Europe and Ireland. Small schooners continued to collect salt from the dock until the 1940s.

The Victoria Dock has three warehouses: Victoria (1849), Britannia (1861) and Albert (1851). These were built for the merchant William Partridge. The Britannia suffered a devastating fire in 1987 and was subsequently rebuilt (in facsimile) in 1988–89 by Dyer Associates.

At the south end of the dock, a 10-ton manually operated crane was installed in around 2007. It came from the former (Midland operated) railway yard at New Mills Station, Cheshire. It was built in 1902 and was saved by members of the National Waterways Museum.

'The Snail'

'The Snail' is the name given to the disused centrifugal water pump that can be seen on the west side of the Main Basin. It was built in 1964 and was capable of pumping 47,000 gallons each minute. The pump was in operation from 1834–2001 and was used to maintain the water supply of the canal by pumping water from the River Severn. The Gloucester and Sharpness Canal has five natural feeders, including the River Cam and the River Frome.

The Dock Mills

The importance of Gloucester to transport goods by river and sea was enhanced by the completion of the Gloucester and Sharpness Canal in 1827. This, along with the repeal of the Corn Laws in 1846, allowed large volumes of imported grain to come into Gloucester. The population of Britain was rapidly expanding during 1750–1850 and, consequently, the demand for flour remained high. It soon became apparent to mill owners that considerable savings in the production costs were possible if transportation and handling expenditure were reduced. For example, grain imported into Gloucester was transhipped, often by canal, to various mills, such as John Biddle's in Stroud. The advent of steam-powered mills allowed them to be located nearer to the source of imported grain and so reduce costs.

'The Snail'.

The City Flour Mills.

The first flour mill, built in the vicinity of the docks, was the Gloucester Steam Mill, constructed around 1840. This was followed by the City Flour Mills, in 1850, which was built by two brothers, Joseph and Jonah Hadley. Their mill is located near Victoria Dock and fronts on to Commercial Road. Initially, the Hadley brothers began milling on a modest scale using a small steam engine to drive two pairs of stones, but so successful were their endeavours that they installed two larger steam engines and, in 1853, built the adjoining warehouse.

In the same year, the crankshaft on one of the steam engines was fractured and needed to be sent back to the manufacturers in Greenwich, so that a pattern for the new one could be made. However, the broken crankshaft was held up in transit and the Hadley brothers sued the courier for loss of profits caused by the delay. The resulting court case, referred to as Hadley v. Baxendale, was a landmark in British legal history, for it ruled that damages resulting from breach of contract should be taken into consideration of what might reasonably have been contemplated by both parties. A plaque, on the mill, commemorates the case.

Over the following decades, more steam mills were constructed at Gloucester, including the Quay Street Mills, established by Samuel Luker. Luker was milling at Grove Mill, Painswick, but clearly saw that the future lay in steam mills located next to good transport links. The City Mills were later taken over by Reynolds and Allen but trade fluctuations caused them to close in 1885. A year later, the mills were taken over by Priday, Metford and Co. Shortly afterwards, there was a fire in the company's adjoining warehouse, which was consequently rebuilt to a greater height by architect J.P. Moore, in 1888–90.

Milling flour in and around Gloucester Docks continued throughout the twentieth century, although work was concentrated in two mills: City Mills, operated by Priday Metford Ltd; and Albert Mills, which was established by James Reynolds in 1869. Albert Mills continued to produce flour until 1977, when it closed. By this time, grain was moved to the mills along the roads rather than transported on the waterways. Priday Metford continued to operate their mill until March 1994 and the City Mills were converted into apartments in 2004.

Foster Brothers' Oil and Cake Mill

Foster Brothers' Oil and Cake Mill is, at the time of writing, derelict, despite the recent development of much of the area into the Gloucester Quays Outlet. The mill, which fronts the Gloucester and Sharpness Canal, was established in 1864 by two brothers, Richard Gibbs Foster and Thomas Nelson Foster, after a fire at their former premises in Evesham, Worcestershire. It continued to be managed by three generations of the Foster family until 1945.

The original premises were designed by George Hunt of Evesham and comprised a six-storey warehouse, with the machinery housed in an extension behind the main structure. From 1891–93, a major expansion took place. The mill was housed in a single-storey building and a detached boiler house was also built to contain the 400hp Hicks-Hargreaves steam engine. During the rebuild, the quay well in front of the warehouses started to subside, threatening the building and particularly the pillars that supported the elevator housing. The company took the step of taking this part of the building down and rebuilding it.

Foster Brothers' Oil and Cake Mill.

The company joined with sixteen other firms, in 1899, to form the British Oil and Cake Mills (BOCM), which, in turn, was taken over by Lever Brothers in 1925. The work was transferred to a new mill at Avonmouth and the site closed in 1955. Following closure, the site was bought by West Midlands Farmer as a distribution depot for products being sent to local farmers. During the 1970s, grain was delivered to the site by coaster. Operations ceased during the 1980s, causing the site's dereliction.

The Railways Around the Docks

The docks were once connected by an intricate network of railway lines to facilitate the movement of goods through the inland port. Although in recent years, much of the old railway infrastructure has been removed, significant remnants of the lines remain and speak of a once-bustling port. These remnants include: sections of railway line left *in situ*, a derelict swing bridge, a preserved steam crane and a former office building.

The docks were first linked by a tramway (*see* Gloucester and Cheltenham Railway p. 90). The arrival of the Birmingham and Gloucester Railway, in 1840, caused the building of a 250yd spur from the station to the horse-worked tramway. By 1845, some 45,000 tons were carried over this section of tramline. However, not all the cargo arriving at the docks was suitable for being transported by the tramway because of the line's tight curves. The obvious solution to the tramway's shortcomings was the building of a railway line to the docks. The first railway facility to be established in the vicinity was the Midland Railway's High Orchard Goods Yard, located at the southern end of Bakers Quay. It opened fully in 1846, but part of the line serving the yard was in use earlier. In September 1847, a tragic accident took place on the line when a locomotive passed along the tracks without an ash-box fitted. A number of smouldering cinders were strewn across a line that was used by the public as a footpath and, shortly after the train had passed, Ann Williams (aged 6) started playing with some embers. Whilst she did so, however, another cinder set light to her frock, with fatal consequences.

The Midland Railway extended their operations in 1900 by opening another branch to the canal. This line ran from Tuffley Junction to Hempstead Wharf. Later this line was extended across Monk Meadow to the Great Western Railway (GWR) Docks line. Traces of this line can still be discerned in the landscape, particularly near to the (still extant) railway bridge that takes the Bristol Road over the course of the line.

The GWR gained access to the docks from a branch that ran from Over Junction and across Alney Island to the newly constructed quay wall at Llanthony. A railway yard was built during the 1860s and Gloucester College stands on this site today. The biggest engineering challenge on the line was the construction of Llanthony Railway Bridge, located just upstream of Llanthony Lock, on the East Parting of the River Severn. The Railway Companies Act specified that the bridge needed to be at least 50ft wide to allow for the passage of boats. Also, in order to access the quay at Llanthony, the bridge needed to cross the river at an angle of nearly 30 degrees. Isambard Kingdom Brunel came up with a solution and designed a swinging span with 103ft-long iron girders supported on timber piles. The swing bridge is thought to have been the first of its kind to use hydraulic power. Most swing bridges at this time had their weight carried completely by a ring at wheels, thus a long, heavy span would have been very difficult to turn. The use of the hydraulic press lifted the span, reducing the load on the wheels, and made the bridge easier to turn.

In September 1853, the strength of the newly built bridge was tested when a GWR locomotive, with railway officials aboard, passed slowly over the bridge. Also at the scene, merchants, and other interested parties gathered to witness the first journey across the bridge. No movement was detected in the structure and more trials were held at gradually increasing speeds, up to around 20mph. The trial of the bridge was evidently considered a success and the gentlemen involved with the trials retired afterwards to a nearby cottage for campaign and other refreshments, whilst the navvies who had worked on the project were given earthenware pitchers full of beer.

The first major project on the bridge took place in 1890–91, and the wooden piles supporting the pivot of the bridge were replaced with two large cast-iron cylinders. In 1899, the replacement of the superstructure with a riveted steel span took place. At the time, Fredrick Wood – master of the trow *Finis* – alleged that the hydraulic machinery was in disrepair, making the opening of the bridge a long and arduous task. Because of this, the yard foreman refused to swing the bridge open, so that when Wood came upriver on a large tide, he had to wait for the water level to drop to get his vessel under the bridge. These allegations were denied by the GWR general manager. Whatever the reasons for the replacement of the superstructure, the new span opened for the first time on 26 December 1899. Vessels continued to use this part of the river until the 1920s, albeit with decreasing regularity. For example, in 1910, there were about 100 movements on the river, but by 1920, that number had reduced to around thirty vessels per year. The last recorded time that the bridge was swung was 8 August 1922. Two years later, all river traffic on this section of the river ceased when movement was detected in one of the walls of Llanthony Lock, necessitating beams to be placed across the lock to stop it from collapsing.

During the rebuilding of the bridge, it was suggested that a walkway supported on brackets should be placed on one side to give access to the lock keeper's cottage at Llanthony Lock. However, GWR would not allow anything that would put extra weight on the bridge. Consequently, in 1908, the opportunity arose to build a private footbridge to the lock. It was constructed from two lattice railway girders, bought second-hand from the railway company, and can still be seen today. During the Second World War, a footbridge was attached to Llanthony Railway Bridge in order to provide a convenient access to Castlemeads Power Station, a small coal-fired station that operated between 1941 and 1969. This footbridge was constructed by Tubewrights of Newport.

Llanthony Yard continued to be busy throughout the twentieth century. Although goods imported directly from the canal declined after the First World War, the yard became an important distribution centre. Following rationalisation of the railway network in the 1960s, traffic over the Llanthony Docks branch consisted mainly of trains for the Blue Circle Cement Depot (which was once located in Llanthony Yard), plus occasional freights bound for the grain silo at Monk Meadow. This traffic gradually declined, with regular traffic ceasing in

A railway wagon on an isolated section of track, near to Llanthony Warehouse.

Llanthony railway branch swing bridge (now derelict). The footbridge to the Llanthony lock keepers cottage can be seen in the background

early 1989 and the yard closed around a year later. The bridge is, at the time of writing, derelict and closed to members of the public because of its condition.

Llanthony Railway Bridge is not the only visible reminder of this branch line. Much of the line across Alney Island is now part of the National Cycle Network after the track was lifted in the 1990s. Llanthony Yard was mostly demolished to make way for newer buildings. However, the former yard offices are now a crèche for Gloucester College. The intricate network of lines that existed around the docks is still partially extant. Even after resurfacing, many of the steel lines around the docks have been left *in situ*. Opposite the lock warehouse at the end of the main basin, resting on an isolated section of track, stands a steam crane. It was used for the lifting of heavy loads from vessels. Built by Joseph Booth & Brothers in Leeds, it dates from 1944.

The Mariners' Chapel

The Mariners' Chapel was built to serve the community around the docks. Before its construction, visiting sailors were encouraged to visit one of the local parish churches, but were often reluctant to do so, on account that they lacked Sunday best – smart clothes that the general populace saved for wearing to church on a Sunday. In order that the dockworkers and seamen might be encouraged to attend a place of divine worship on a Sunday, a number of merchants and other publically spirited citizens funded the building of the chapel.

The chapel's simple design is by John Jacques and the single-cell structure was built in the late thirteenth-century style, complete with lancets and a bell-cote. The sanctuary is located at the west end of the building (as opposed to the more usual east end) owing to its close proximity to Sturge's Warehouse. The building work was undertaken by William Wingate, a local builder, and began in 1848.

The Mariners' Chapel.

The Revd James Hollins was appointed as the first chaplain and the inaugural service as held on 11 February 1849. At this time, the chaplain would visit each ship after it had docked and would also call at sailor's homes in order to spread the message of Christianity and to attend to their spiritual needs. The chaplain also organised foreign-language services, established a Sunday school for the boatmen's children and exhorted those he came into contact with to give up drink and gambling. The nucleus of the congregation came from the dock labourers and their families. During the first five years of ministry at the chapel, 2,000 copies of the Bible were distributed.

The chapel is still in use as a place of worship and continues to welcome many visitors. Modern stained-glass windows (created 1996–2000) by Gerald Paxton and Michelle Butler have been inserted to mark the 150th anniversary of the opening of the chapel and the 200th anniversary of the docks. The other, older, stained-glass windows came, originally, from St Catherine's church, which was demolished in 1921 (see St Oswald's Priory p. 40). These windows are by Clayton and Bell.

The Spa

The cluster of regency buildings around Spa Road owes much to the creation of the Gloucester Spa. In 1814, workmen were digging a well in Rigney Stile Grounds, located to the south east of the city, when they discovered a saline chalybeate spring at a depth of 80ft (24.4m). The landowner, banker Sir James Jelf, immediately saw the potential for developing the area as a fashionable spa resort. On 1 May 1815 a pump room, with surrounding walks, was opened. The treatment rooms boasted the latest in hot and cold vapour treatments and three pumps connected the three sources of the water of varying strengths. It was claimed that the waters had strong purgative effects and that they were also good for kidney disorders, gastric or acid indigestion, gall bladder obstruction, nausea and jaundice. Two prominent chemists tested the waters. The first was Sir Charles Daubeny, a professor of chemistry at Oxford, who carried out an examination of the waters and concluded that they had a high iodine content. The other

was Fredrick Accum, a German chemist, appointed as a royal apothecary in 1793, who concluded that the spring contained more life-giving properties than any other spring in the country so far. Accum was an advocate of using gas for lighting and wrote a number of books on chemistry. However, in 1820, he had a spectacular reversal of fortune when he was discovered tearing leaves from books in the Royal Institution Library. The managers of the library pursued legal action, first on a charge of robbery and then on the charge that he had mutilated library books. Accum became a subject of ridicule and moved back to Germany before the case could be heard in court.

Nos 13–15 Spa Road. Formerly The Spa Hotel.

James Jelf's bank was caught up in a national banking crisis following the end of the war with France and he was declared bankrupt. Local investors raised £6,500 to purchase the Gloucester Spa Company and plots of land around the spa were sold off to developers. Prominent buyers included William Hicks (a builder), John Chadborn (a solicitor) and John Phillpotts (a barrister and later an MP). They and others are responsible for many of the regency buildings in the area. No. 1 Spa Road dates from roughly 1820 and sets the 'Cheltenham-like' appearance of the street. The Spa Hotel, Nos 13–15, was built by the Spa Company as a 'commodious and extensive boarding house' in 1818 and was enlarged in 1851 by Jacques and Sons. Later the building became a girls' school, Ribston Hall. Maitland House, No. 17, was built in around 1820 by Thomas Rickman for Alexander Maitland, a banker. The house is now a register office. The Judges' Lodgings

were built for John Phillpotts by Sir Robert Smirke in about 1825, as a 'spacious and elegant mansion'. It was originally called Somerset House and became the Judges' Lodgings after it was converted to lodgings for assize court judges. It is a distinctive building with a wrought-iron veranda and a delicate first-floor tented balcony.

Work began on Brunswick Square in 1822 and nineteen three-storey houses were completed by 1825. The remainder of the planned development was never completed, however, and it was decided to leave the central area as a garden. Brunswick Square was built on an area just outside the old city walls known as Gaudy Green and was used for archery practice by local bowmen until the seventeenth century. Royalist Artillery were also stationed here in 1643, during the Siege of Gloucester.

The Spa Company was also responsible for the construction of the Beaufort Buildings,

Maitland House.

Brunswick Square.

The Judges' Lodgings.

which were begun in 1818 as a speculative development. The development consists of a long stuccoed terrace of three storeys with Ionic porticoes and some wrought-iron work. Herbert Vaughan (1832–1903), a cardinal of Westminster from 1892 until his death, was born here.

In 1861, the spa was given over to the City Corporation. However, it was little patronised.

The pump room baths fell into disrepair and, consequently, were closed in 1894. In 1926, the medicinal springs were closed after they had become contaminated. The Spa Pump Room, a pretty building dating from 1815, was demolished in 1960, after it too was allowed to fall into disrepair. The pump room had a veranda and a parapet decorated with carved lions and acorn vases.

Over Bridge

Over Bridge was opened in 1831. The design, by Thomas Telford, was based on Jean-Rodolphe Perronet's (former) Pont de Neuilly, which was built across the River Seine, near Paris, in 1768. The 150ft (45.7m) single span of the Over Bridge crosses the west parting of the River Severn. Despite the fact that the crown arch sank 10in on the removal of the centering, the bridge carried road traffic until 1974.

Thomas Telford's Over Bridge.

Addison's Folly

Addison's Folly, built for the lawyer Thomas Fenn Addison, stands at the end of a passage called Marylone, close to St Mary de Crypt church. The Grade II listed building, which dates from 1864, consists of the surviving portion of an Italianate-style house with an attached three-stage rectangular tower. The folly was built as a memorial to Robert Raikes, the founder of the Sunday school movement. From the top of the tower, it is possible to see St Swithun's church, Hempstead, 1.5 miles away. This is where Addison's wife, Hannah, lies buried, and this may further explain why the tower was built.

Addison's Folly.

Nos 19 and 21 Eastgate Street

From the late 1880s, a general economic revival allowed the expansion of banking in Gloucester's economy. The growth of the banking sector left its mark on the city and is evidenced in the grand Lloyd's Bank (No. 19 Eastgate Street), which was designed by F.W. Waller and erected in 1898. It was built in the Flemish Renaissance style, consisting of rusticated granite with large, round arches above doors and windows. Above this, the building is made of red brick with terracotta dressings.

The NatWest Bank (No. 21 Eastgate Street) is a similarly impressive building. It was designed by Charles Gribble of London, with Ionic columns at ground level, and built in 1888–89. Inside, a preserved piece of relaid Roman mosaic, uncovered when the bank was built, is displayed in the hall.

Barnwood Park and Arboretum

Barnwood Park and Arboretum are the remainder of the Barnwood House Estate, which was also, for a number of years, a private asylum. The first Barnwood House was built in 1800–05 by Robert Morris (of Barnwood Court) for his son, Robert Morris Junior. However, Robert Morris Junior preferred to live in Cheltenham and the house was sold to Sir Charles Hotham.

Barnwood Park. The former chapel can just be seen behind the trees.

In 1811, Sir Charles died and his memorial can be found on the north wall of the nave in Gloucester Cathedral. His widow remarried a year later and the property was sold. Barnwood House was bought by David Walters and, in 1833, the property was inherited by his son, John Woodbridge Walters. Around this time, Wotton Brook, which flows through the estate, was dammed to form the ponds that can still be seen today. John Woodbridge Walters died in 1852, leaving large debts; consequently, Barnwood House was sold to a consortium that wished to establish a private asylum.

In 1858–60, the building was expanded by local architects Fulljames and Waller, adding two new wings to house patients. Much of the landscaping was completed at this time and bridges built over Wotton Brook allowed patients to complete a circular walk. On the park side of Barnwood Park and Arboretum, a noticeable dip indicates the line of an original path. In addition, some unusual tree species were planted, which now form part of the arboretum.

In 1869, a chapel, designed by F.S. Waller, was added to the site. The chapel is rock-faced in a Gothic style, with an apse at the east end. In 1887, a south aisle was added. Today, this former chapel is used as a gym. F.S. Waller also designed the replacement for the original Barnwood House, which had fallen into disrepair. The replacement building was erected between 1896 and 1897 and remained in use until the hospital fell into decline during the twentieth century, finally closing in 1968. Subsequently, most of the hospital was demolished, apart from the central block of Barnwood House, which became a private residence. This too was demolished in 2001 for redevelopment and the land was given to Gloucester City Council. In 2002, the council built a new bridge linking the arboretum and the park.

The asylum was home to a number of well-known patients over the years. The poet and composer, Ivor Gurney (see Ivor Gurney pp. 116–17), stayed here for a short time in 1922, and Spike Milligan is also thought to have been a patient.

Herbert Vaughan

Herbert Alfred Henry Joseph Thomas Vaughan was born at Beaufort Buildings, Gloucester. He was the eldest of thirteen children born to Colonel John Francis Vaughan (1808–80) and Elizabeth Louisa Rolls (1810–53). At the age of 16, Vaughan expressed a desire to serve in the priesthood and, following his training, he was ordained on 28 October 1854. In 1857, he became a founding member of the Order of St Charles and, having been encouraged to establish a house to train priests for foreign missionary work, he founded St Joseph's College at Mill Hill in London in 1866. Vaughan was appointed Bishop of Salford in 1872 and became Archbishop of Westminster in 1892, following the death of Archbishop Henry Edward Manning. Two years later, in 1894, Vaughan appointed John Francis Bentley as architect to design Westminster Cathedral. A Byzantine style was selected so that the outer shell of the building could be erected quickly and because it was cost effective. Vaughan died on 19 June 1903 and enough of the cathedral had been completed for Vaughan's Requiem Mass to be held there, followed by his burial at St Joseph's College on 26 June 1903.

Eastgate Market
Portico.

Eastgate Market Portico

In 1855–56, the Eastgate Market Portico was built by Medland and Maberley, to the west of its present location. The portico contains many fine carvings. These include the figures of Ceres and Father Time by Henry Frith, which flank the clock above the entrance. There are also carvings above the archways that show market produce. The portico was moved to its present location in 1973, when Shingler Risdon Associates built the new Eastgate Market Hall between 1968 and 1974.

Eight

THE TWENTIETH CENTURY: THE AGE OF INVENTION, ART AND RESILIENCE

Ivor Gurney and Gloucester

GLOUCESTER CONTAINS a number of landmarks connected with poet and composer Ivor Gurney. He was born on 28 August 1890, the eldest son of David and Florence Gurney, and the family lived at No. 3 Queen Street, Gloucester, where David Gurney was the proprietor of a tailoring business. Ivor's godfather was Revd Alfred Hunter Cheesman, the vicar of St Matthew's church, Twigworth. Cheesman was a source of encouragement to the young Gurney and allowed him access to his large library.

Gurney was a chorister of Gloucester Cathedral and was educated at the cathedral's King's School. Afterwards, he was an articled pupil of A. Herbert Brewer, the cathedral's organist. At this time, Gurney took up a number of posts as organist to a variety of churches in Gloucestershire, including the Mariner's Chapel, located in

Gloucester Docks. In 1911, he won a scholarship to study at the Royal College of Music, under Charles Villers Stanford.

Following the outbreak of the First World War in 1914, Gurney attempted to enlist but was rejected owing to his poor eyesight. However, on 9 February 1915, Gurney tried again and went on to serve as a private with the 2nd/5th Gloucesters. On Good Friday 1917, Gurney sustained a minor bullet wound and, on 10 September of the same year, he was injured in a gas attack during the third battle of Ypres (Passchendaele). Returning to England, Gurney exhibited signs of mental instability while he was recuperating from his injuries, and he was discharged from the army in October 1918. Gurney continued his studies at the Royal College of Music – this time under Ralph Vaughan Williams – but he found it difficult to concentrate and so returned to Gloucester. Unable to find employment, Gurney lived on a small disability pension and the charity of family and friends.

Although music was now flowing from his pen, his behaviour grew increasingly erratic. In September 1922, Gurney was diagnosed with paranoid schizophrenia and was committed to Barnwood House Asylum (*see* Barnwood Park and Arboretum p. 117). On 21 December of that year, Gurney was transferred to the City of London Mental Hospital, Dartford, Kent. Here, Gurney remained until his death.

Although over 1,700 items of poetry are in existence (and are kept in the Gurney collection of Gloucester Archive), Gurney was only able to publish two volumes of poetry in his lifetime: *Severn and Somme* (1917) and *War's Embers* (1919). These poems reflect his love of the Gloucestershire countryside, deal

Candle by Wulfgang Butress.

The grave of Ivor Gurney,
St Matthew's church, Twigworth.

with the realities of trench warfare, and chart the decline of his mental health. From the 1920s, Gurney's songs also began to be published. These include his two Houseman Cycles, 'Ludlow and Teme' and 'The Western Playland', which were included as part of the Carnegie Collection of British Music in 1923 and 1926 respectively. The music was scored for solo voice, string quartet and piano, which enhanced Gurney's reputation as a composer.

Gurney died from tuberculosis on 26 September 1937 at the City of London

Mental Hospital. His burial took place at St Matthew's church, Twigworth, Gloucester. More collections of music were issued after his death and, in 1938, the Oxford University Press published two volumes containing twenty of Gurney's songs. His friend Marion Scott (1877–1953) saved a number of his manuscripts, which enabled further collections of Gurney's music to be published.

Interest in Ivor Gurney has grown in recent decades and the Ivor Gurney Society, established in 1995, continues to promote research into his life and work. More recently, an artwork by sculptor Wolfgang Buttress was installed in the docks. The work stands 23m high and is made from laser-cut and etched corten rolled steel. It was built in 2010 and can be internally lit. The title of the sculpture, *Candle*, refers to Gurney's poem 'Requiem':

Requiem

Pour out your light, O stars,
    and do not hold
Your loveliest shining from earth's
    outworn shell
Pure and cold are your radiance –
    pure and cold
My dead friend's face as well.

Requiem

Pour out your bounty moon of
    radiant shining
On all this shattered flesh, on all those
    quiet forms;
For these were slain, so quiet reclining
In noblest cause was ever waged
    with arms.

Herbert Cecil Booth and the Invention of the Vacuum Cleaner

Herbert Cecil Booth (1871–1955) was born in Gloucester. The family lived at Theresa Place before moving to Belle Vue House, Spa Road, as recorded on a blue information plaque

Belle Vue House.

on the building. In 1889, he entered the City and Guilds General Institution to study civil engineering on their three-year course. Here, he distinguished himself academically and later became a member of the Institution of Civil Engineers. He was first employed by Maudslay, Sons and Field – the leading marine engineers in the country – and helped to design battleships for the Royal Navy. In 1894, a director of the company, W.B. Basset, asked Booth to work on the designs of a 'Great Wheel' then being constructed in Earl Court. Booth was to sort out the numerous technical problems on the project and design three other wheels for construction in Blackpool, Vienna and Paris. In 1901, he founded his own consultancy company.

Booth got the idea of inventing the vacuum cleaner after seeing a demonstration of an American machine that blew dust from carpets. In 1901, Booth's invention was completed and the British Vacuum Cleaner Company was founded the same year. The early machines were large and had to be horse-drawn. In part this was because the machines had to carry their own coal or oil-powered generators, since few homes had electricity. The machine was used to clean the carpets before the coronation of Edward VII. The king asked for a demonstration at Buckingham Palace and two machines were ordered for there and Windsor.

The Invention of the Jet Engine and Spirit of Aviation Statue

On Northgate Street, at the junction where it meets The Oxbode, stands a statue depicting a man standing on a jet engine, holding both his hands to his ears. The statue, commissioned by Gloucester City Council, was created by sculptor Simon Springer and erected in 1999 to celebrate the achievements of the Gloster Aircraft Company. It is entitled *Spirit of Aviation*.

The Gloster Aircraft Company was founded in 1917 and, during its forty-six year history, the company manufactured some 12,000 aircraft. The Gloster E28/39, constructed in 1940–41, was the first jet-powered aircraft to be built in Britain. The aircraft was made possible by Frank Whittle (1907–96), the inventor of the first British jet engine.

Frank Whittle was born in Coventry, to working-class parents. In September 1923, he was accepted by the RAF at their training college at Cranwell. His outstanding ability meant that Whittle formed part of the 1 per cent of recruits who were promoted to the officer training corps. He was passed out second from Cranwell in July 1928, and posted to 111 Fighter Squadron at Hornchurch. One year later, Whittle was posted to Wittering to begin the RAF's flying instructor's course. It was whilst at Wittering that he conceived the idea of using a gas turbine to produce a

Spirit of Aviation statue.

Detail from the commemorative stone at Brockworth Business Park.

propelling jet. With the help of Flying Officer W.E.P. (Pat) Johnson, who had trained as a patent officer, Whittle was able to patent his idea on 16 January 1939. The Air Ministry showed no interest in Whittle's design, so he took the idea to a number of companies, including British Thompson-Houston, Armstrong Siddley and the Bristol Aeroplane Company. All of these companies were unwilling to invest, however, owing to the prohibitive cost and the lack of suitable materials. Consequently, Whittle continued with his career with the RAF. In 1932, he enrolled on an RAF engineering course near Henlow and gained such outstanding results that he applied to the Air Ministry to be sent to Cambridge University in order to take the mechanical science tripos. His application was successful and he was posted to Cambridge in July 1934.

Whittle was able to keep up his flying through Cambridge University's Air Squadron. During this period, Whittle received a letter from Rolf Dudley-Williams, a fellow cadet from his days at Cranwell, who claimed to have found a financial backer to help develop Whittle's jet engine. The investor was O.T. Folk & Partners, an investment bank, and they advanced Whittle £2,000 to develop proposals and set up Power Jet Ltd to design a prototype engine. Work on the engine was interfering with Whittle's studies and he left the project five weeks prior to his examinations so that he could concentrate fully on passing. It was somewhat to Whittle's surprise that he received a first for his efforts. Following a year's postgraduate research, the RAF placed Whittle on the special operations list, which allowed him to work full-time on developing the jet engine. Development continued at Lutterworth, where British Thompson-Houston had its foundry.

On 30 June 1939, the Director of Scientific Research visited Lutterworth and witnessed a test run of the engine. It ran for twenty-eight minutes and travelled at speeds of up to 16,000rpm. Two weeks after the visit, Power Jet Ltd received a contract for a flight jet engine, British Thompson-Houston for its manufacture and the Gloster Aircraft Company for the manufacture of the experimental aeroplane. A test engine was installed in the E28/39 at Gloucester and, on 7 April 1941, tests were carried out on the Gloster Aircraft Company's airfield at Brockworth, Gloucester. Whittle carried out the first taxiing runs at speeds of up to 60mph, before handing over control of the aircraft to P.E.G. Sayer, the Gloster chief test pilot. After a few preliminary runs, Sayer took the plane to the downwind area of the airfield. On the way back up the airfield, the plane was airborne for a few seconds. Sayer then repeated this a further two times. These first short hops were the first time that a jet-propelled aircraft had been airborne in Britain. The first flight of the E28/39 took place at Lutterworth a month later on 15 May 1941.

Ten hours' worth of flight trials were completed quickly and no problems occurred with the engine or the aircraft. Whittle continued to work on jet engines and one of his designs, the W2/700, was adapted by Rolls-Royce for their Derwent V engine. This engine was installed in a Gloster Meteor and this aircraft won a world airspeed record, in 1945, with a speed of 606mph.

Whittle retired from the RAF in 1948. He received a KBE in the birthday honours list and a Royal Commission award to inventors for £100,000. Whittle continued to receive a number of prizes over the following thirty years. On 9 August 1996, he died in Columbia, Maryland, and his ashes were later interred at RAF Lutterworth.

In addition to the *Spirit of Aviation* statue at Brockworth Business Park (close to the site of the Gloster Aircraft Company) a memorial also records the building of the Gloster E28/39.

James Carne

In the North Ambulatory Chapel, a set of carved crosses are on display. They were carved by James Power Carne (1906–86), an army officer, who was captured and held as a prisoner of war during the Korean War.

Carne was born in Falmouth, Cornwall. He was educated at the Imperial Service College, Windsor, and later studied at the Royal Military College at Sandhurst. He was commissioned into the Gloucestershire Regiment in 1925, and went on to serve with the King's African Rifles. From 1947, Carne lead the 5th (TA) Battalion of the Gloucestershire Regiment. When the 1st Battalion was ordered to Korea, in August 1950, Carne was given orders to command it. Following the end of the Second World War, Korea was a divided nation. The country was split at the 38th parallel: the North was a Soviet-influenced Communist state and the South was a fledgling democracy with support from the United States. On 25 June 1950, North Korean soldiers invaded the South. This provoked a reaction from the United Nations, who raised a force to halt the advance of the North Korean troops. The UN force was commanded by General Douglas MacArthur, who was able to rout the North Korean Army and advance UN troops into the northern territories with the intention of unifying the country. The advance of MacArthur's army into North Korea alarmed the Chinese, who sent experienced troops to drive the UN forces back over the 38th parallel.

Carne was awarded a Distinguished Service Order (DSO) for the way that he handled his battalion at the start of the war. He was also awarded a Victoria Cross for his part in Gloucester's heroic stand on the Imjin River between 22 and 24 April 1951, with his vastly outnumbered force of less than 800 soldiers. The Gloucesters were trying to defend a front of 12,000yds and the attacking Chinese forces outnumbered Carne's by 20 to 1. For three days and three nights the Gloucesters held their line, whilst the enemy rained down unrelenting machine-gun fire. Carne chose to lead by example. He moved quietly about the battlefield, often smoking a pipe, and took command of small assault parties to recover any territory that was lost. After three days, Carne was down to 169 men. Eventually he was told that his troops would not be relieved and he was told to disperse his men and make for the UN line further back. Carne was following these instructions when he was captured, along with the smaller group that he was commanding.

Carne spent the next two years as a prisoner of war in North Korea. The conditions were brutal, and prisoners were subject to starvation, torture and backbreaking work. Lectures aimed at converting the prisoners to Communism were given and any prisoners who relented were offered their freedom (in either North Korea or China). Despite the conditions, very few captured soldiers

Lieutenant Colonel James Power Carne. (Imperial War Museum, ref. 5401-13)

changed their allegiance. During his captivity, Carne and another officer were convicted of having a 'generally hostile' attitude towards Communism; they were sentenced to solitary confinement. Carne preserved his sanity by carving stone crosses.

Eventually, after two years, Carne and his fellow prisoners were released and returned to England; they received a heroes' welcome on arrival at Southampton on 15 October 1953. Carne received a number of awards and honours after he was released. He received the American Distinguished Service Cross and was granted the Freedom of Gloucester. The following year he was granted the Freedom of Falmouth. Carne spoke little about his captivity in North Korea, simply stating that: 'I have gained an added pride in being British and have lost a little weight.' He retired from the army in 1957, and went to live in Cranham, Gloucestershire. He died on 19 April 1986 and was buried at St James' church, Cranham. The crosses that he carved whilst in North Korea were later presented to Gloucester Cathedral and placed in the North Ambulatory Chapel, which forms part of Gloucester Cathedral's memorial chapel, dedicated to those who have suffered because of conflict.

BIBLIOGRAPHY

Amphlett, D.G., *Not A Guide To Gloucester* (Brimscombe: The History Press, 2012).

Bagshaw, Richard W., *Roman Roads* (Alesbury: Shire Publications, 1979).

Bick, David E., *The Gloucester and Cheltenham Railway: and the Leckhampton Quarry Tramroads* (Lingfield: Oakwood Press, 1968).

Booth, Frank, *Robert Raikes of Gloucester* (Redhill: National Christian Education Centre, 1980).

Conway-Jones, Hugh, *Gloucester Docks: An Historical Guide* (Lydney: Black Dwarf Publications, 2008).

Davies, Hugh, *Roads in Roman Britain* (Stroud: Tempus, 2002).

Herbert, N.M., *A History of the County of Gloucester*, Vol. 4 (Oxford University Press, 1988).

Maggs, Colin G., *Branch Lines of Gloucestershire* (Sutton, 1991)

Margary, Ivan Donald, *Roman Roads in Britain* (John Baker, 1967).

Mills Stephen and Pierce Riemer, *The Mills of Gloucestershire* (Buckingham: Barracuda, 1983).

Morris, Robert, *The Siege of Gloucester 1643* (Bristol: Stuart Press, 1993).

Moss, Philip, *Historic Gloucester: An Illustrated Guide to the City and its Buildings* (Brimscombe: The History Press, 2009).

Scarre, Christopher, *Chronicle of Emperors: The Reign-by-Reign Record of the Rulers of Imperial Rome* (London: Thames and Hudson, 1995).

Sullivan, Pete, *A Gloucester Martyr: John Hooper and the English Reformation* (Bakewell: Country Books, 2004).

Verey, David and Alan Brooks, *The Buildings of England: Gloucestershire 2: The Vale and the Forest of Dean* (London: Yale University Press, 2002).

Walters, Thomas B., *Robert Raikes* (Epworth Press, 1930).

Warmington, Alan, *Civil War, Interregnum and Restoration in Gloucestershire, 1640–1672* (London: Royal Historical Society, 1997)

Witts, Chris, *A Century of Bridges* (Gloucester: River Severn Publications, 1998, 2nd edition).

INDEX

Also from The History Press

FADING ADS

Take a photographic journey into an often overlooked advertising history and see how a region's businesses of old made use of hand-painted signs to inform, advertise and appeal to consumers. Richly illustrated, this series reveals the many varied industries, businesses and companies of yesteryear that now appear faded – like ghosts – on the brickwork of buildings. It is a snapshot of a time that is almost forgotten but which lives on through the sometimes haunting presence of ghost signs on the streets and buildings we walk past.

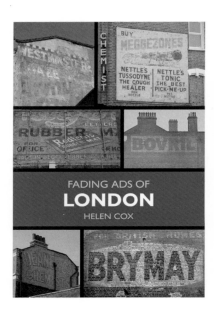

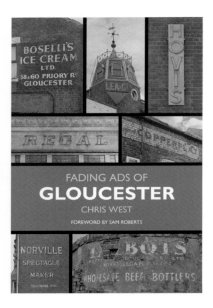